Life at My Fingertips

Life at My Fingertips

Robert J. Smithdas

DOUBLEDAY & COMPANY, INC., GARDEN CITY, NEW YORK

1958

Library of Congress Catalog Card Number 58–7369

DEDICATION

To my beloved mother and father, who gave me life and love, who watched over me and encouraged my hopes and dreams with unfailing understanding, this book is dedicated with a heart full of eternal gratitude.

CONTENTS

Introduction

THE AUTOBIOGRAPHY of Robert Smithdas is a moving testament to personal courage and the dramatic potentialities of the human mind. Nearly twelve years have passed since Robert became my very dear friend and associate in our work for the deaf and blind; yet as intimately as I have come to know him, I still feel it difficult to appreciate fully the immensity of the victory he has won. His story has given me new insight into his never-ending struggle to penetrate still further the silent fog that once threatened to blot out all contact with the outer world. In reading this book I seemed to undergo with Robert his experience of blindness and deafness and feel his responses to the problems they present. With him I have lived in a world known only by touch, smell, and taste.

I read Robert's autobiography with one great advantage —if I did not personally know the extent of his struggles, I am at least acquainted with the extent of his victory. I want to tell the reader a little of the man Robert has made of himself. At thirty-three he is a poised young individual who seems never to be at a loss in whatever company he finds himself. He combines to an unusual degree qualities of curiosity, sensitivity, and imagination, and with them an extraordinary sense of humor and fantasy. The reader will discover, perhaps to his surprise, that Robert writes about his extraordinary adjustment step by step to the world around him not only with frankness but also with considerable humor.

I would like to bear personal testimony to the skills Robert has acquired. His sense of touch seems almost magical. It is developed to the point where he can combine a reasonable whole out of unreasonable, fragmentary parts. I have seen Robert create an uncannily accurate personality picture out of a simple handshake with a stranger. And I want to add a comment on his voice. Although he hasn't any idea what it sounds like, day after day on his lecture tours for our I.H.B. he thrills audiences he will never see. In spite of his handicaps he has trained his voice to carry out all the exacting requirements of a finished public speaker.

Robert has told his story in his own fashion, sometimes using language that only he with his limited contact with the world would have employed. Yet his meaning is at all times unmistakable. In his poetry as well as his prose significant flashes of his inner life appear. No one else, for instance, could have written the lines to his *Spring Advent*:

> My eyes are closed; yet somehow without knowing,
> My senses guess what beauty lies between
> This sunlit nook and those far hills throwing
> Bright spears of color where blank snows have been.
> Now suddenly the air is stirred with wonder
> As spring comes bursting in like silent thunder.

The autobiography of Robert Smithdas, I believe, conveys this sense of silent thunder—not the thunder of spring, but the thunder of unusual courage and defiance of adversity.

On behalf of the I.H.B. I would like to express thanks for

all those who had a hand in the preparation of this book. We especially would like to thank Dana Lee Thomas, the biographer, who first broached the conception of this book to us and who has worked with Robert, editing, guiding the material, and stimulating him to clarify the best of his thinking and feeling for these pages. We should also like to thank Mrs. Madeline Jacobs, director of the braille transcribing service at the National Braille Press, Boston, Massachusetts, who directed the brailling of this manuscript, enabling Robert to check and edit the text. We would further express our gratitude to Mr. George E. Keane, Director of Community Relations at the I.H.B., for his encouragement and counsel at many points during the preparation of this book.

PETER J. SALMON, Executive Director
Industrial Home for the Blind, Brooklyn, N.Y.

I praise my God, for He has guided me
Through darkness too intense to find the day:
I praise my God, for He provided me
With music when all sound had died away.

Out of the depths of silence too profound,
Out of the depths of darkness and despair,
My soul has risen through the world and found
A thousand blessings in His loving care.

Into the songless darkness of my days
The light of hope and song of love have crept,
Until my spirit sings this hymn of praise
To Him who woke me when my whole life slept.

ROBERT JOSEPH SMITHDAS

Life at My Fingertips

Chapter I

The Curtain Is Lowered

I WAS five when I was stricken with cerebral spinal meningitis that took away my sight and hearing. I remember the occasion vividly. It was a morning in early summer. The sunshine flooded the lawns and terraces of Sunnyland Street, Pittsburgh, where I lived. I had been playing by myself, wandering up and down in front of the buff and red brick houses, chasing June bugs and butterflies.

I recall to this hour the large gray cat with yellow eyes that was stretched out lazily on a porch across the street from my home. I have never been partial to cats and this one, with its large proportions, especially frightened me. I would look at it with fascination, but nothing would induce me to go near enough to touch its shining gray fur. I wondered what would happen if it suddenly sprang to life and pursued me.

It was noon when my mother called me for lunch. The picture has remained with me in all its vividness. Mother came out to the yard and stood behind the hedge, hands on hips. She wore a light print dress; her brown hair was swept backward over her head and bound in a large bun at the nape of her neck.

I was a rebellious child. Even though it was time for my nap, I was reluctant to leave the sunshine. I protested that I did not feel at all tired. But mother insisted that I come inside. My noonday snack consisted of a glass of foaming milk and a thick slice of homemade bread and butter. This was during the Depression, when it was cheaper to make bread at home than buy it in the store. One of my happiest memories is the appearance of the crust, a crisp, light-brown substance that seemed to have a faint tint of gold impregnating it.

The kitchen was a spacious room painted in blue and white. Scarlet geraniums stood on the window sill in clay pots; and the tender green shoots of onion bulbs emerged from wineglasses filled with water.

After lunch was over I went to the living room. The curtains were drawn; the room had the dusky light that made one feel drowsy. Lying on the sofa, tracing in the air the design of the flowers on the wallpaper overhead, I gradually fell asleep. I have no recollection of how long I slept. When I awoke I felt a sharp stabbing pain in the center of my back, running up and down my spine. It was as though someone were thrusting needles deep into my flesh. I cried out, "Mommy, something is hurting my back!"

Within seconds my mother was bending over, asking what was troubling me. A few filtered rays of sunlight sifted in through the curtains, playing across her face. Then everything began to fade. I felt myself sinking into the darkness, still crying out with pain, wondering what was happening to me. Nothing is clear after this. I awoke only once to find myself folded in my mother's arms; we were in a car with two other people and I caught a glimpse of houses and trees flashing past the windows. The pain was gone; there was only the sensation of being very tired and weak.

Afterwards I discovered that I had spent nearly three months in the hospital. During most of this time I was unconscious. On a few occasions, I was roused sufficiently to notice trivial things—a nurse in a blue and white uniform bending over me; and once, I think I saw a white pitcher and a glass standing on a tray. These were the last visible signs of the normal world in which I had lived and played.

When I finally regained consciousness long enough to concentrate on my environment I found myself huddled on a thick feather quilt. Nothing seemed familiar. I could not remember where I had been or what had happened. I thought that it was night; but where was the darkness? I remember rubbing my eyes, trying to erase the film of drowsiness that clung to me like a mist. The darkness was neither black nor gray, but a thick muddy fog.

My hands groped around me. My mother, who must have been watching me, spoke close to my ear, very slowly and distinctly. I felt the touch of her lips.

"Bobby, are you all right?"

I wanted to know where I was, why I was no longer able to see around me.

"You are home, darling, safe with Mommy and Daddy. Everything will be fine again."

I could sense, somehow, that my mother was crying, ever so quietly. When I placed my fingers on her eyes I felt their wetness. I could not understand why she should cry.

As I spoke to her, the sound of my voice babbled in my right ear, but I could not understand what I was saying. I did not know that I was blind or that I had lost the total hearing of my left ear and most of the hearing in my right one. Even if I had been told that I was blind and steadily growing deaf, it wouldn't have made any impression upon me. With my awakening into sightlessness, my feeling was merely one of wonder. There was no fear. How could I be afraid of what I could not understand?

I stretched out my hand uncertainly and touched an object. As I began to run my fingers over its surface I gradually recalled its shape and recognized it. It was one of our kitchen chairs. I gripped it, drew myself to my knees, and tried to stand erect. But I slipped backward into the feather quilt.

The weeks that immediately followed are wrapped in an impenetrable haze. I had no sense of time. I would sleep at irregular hours and dream of things that belonged to the world I had left. I would dream of brown fields and bright stars in the sky, of sunbeams sparkling in the April rain. I would see again the faces of my mother and father, the dearest people of all. The most insignificant scenes would come back to me with startling vividness. Once again I would be playing in the back yard with my sister, Ruth, two years older than I, and her friend, Lois. We would be rolling chunks of snow into blocks for a snow man. My hands were smaller than the girls' and, while Ruth and Lois were able to pack solid blocks, the snow invariably crumbled to pieces in my grip, and hot tears of frustration poured down my cheeks. And there were other memories, too: the funeral procession I held to bury my dead canary; the grave I dug solemnly in our back yard, behind the hedge; the drooping flower planted on its resting place. These memories have not faded with the years. Like great roots that cling to the earth, they keep me linked to the life I shall never forget.

During this period of torpor the only incident I can recall from the present world was my struggle to walk again.

During my illness my left leg had become swollen by an infection and the doctors were on the point of amputating it. However, they finally succeeded in draining out most of the fluid through a large incision in my ankle. For several weeks I was badly crippled, and I stumbled about by clinging to anything that would support me.

For six months after my illness I was unable to distinguish between night and day except by the vibratory movements of the people around me, the warmth of the sun on my face. Time had no meaning. Life was simply a continuous physical rhythm. This period must have been a trying one for my parents. Sometimes I would awaken at night shouting for food. On other occasions, since I had no conception of the hour, I would refuse to go to sleep, insisting that it was still daylight. On several occasions my father, hearing me scream for ice cream at two in the morning, would sleepily get into his clothes and go searching for a drugstore that might still be open, to pacify me. At other times when my mother, placing her lips on my right ear, said, "Bobby, it is time to wake up and eat breakfast," I would scream with clenched fists that it didn't matter what time one ate his breakfast. It was a long while before I was able to establish the habit of placing my actions in a time sequence.

It is a curious fact that when I finally learned to distinguish between day and night, I developed an acute fear of darkness. It is difficult to explain why I should have been afraid of the dark when I could not see it. Yet, whenever the warmth of the sun left my face, and I realized night was coming on, I would cling to anyone who happened to be at hand. If I found myself alone when night began I would feel a chill creeping along my spine and hurry to where I knew there was light. Nights as I lay in bed waiting for sleep

I would break into a sweat, convinced that someone was lurking in the shadows to do me harm. I would dive beneath the blankets, pulling them about my body.

In time, I began to recognize the familiar people and objects around me. We had wooden floors in our home and the vibrations of footsteps were quite pronounced. When somebody approached me in my bedroom the footsteps shook the iron legs of my bed, causing the metal to palpitate. I shivered when I heard the vibrations of my mother's vacuum cleaner. I found the vibrations of refrigerators disturbing.

Possessed with an insatiable curiosity about everyone and everything, I stumbled about the house like a wild animal, bumping into chairs, bureaus, bruising my face and arms and shins. At times my mother would exclaim in exasperation, "Bobby, stop feeling things!" But to be reproached only made me more determined. Instead of continuing my probings openly, I would make certain that I was alone in the room before proceeding.

Drawers and closets held fascinating secrets. I would open a closet, explore every article of clothing and hardware. I would sniff at these, feel the textures, trace the designs and shapes. If I could not recognize their uses I would ask one of my sisters to explain them to me. This passion for probing extended to my father's tools, my sisters' cosmetics, and the paraphernalia to be found in kitchen closets. I was in the habit of sampling the preserves and other foodstuffs my mother stored on her shelves. I believe I have tasted almost every ingredient that goes into ordinary cooking, including baking soda, yeast, lard, and other unpleasant foodstuffs. Because flowers usually had enticing aromas, I would often nibble at their petals until I learned to differentiate between them. The only flower, incidentally, that I ever found really palatable was the nasturtium; it had a strong tangy flavor that was not wholly unfavorable.

Occasionally, I barely missed having a serious accident. Once I managed to swing myself up to the shelf of an old cabinet. It tipped slightly and I was forced to come down in a hurry. When my feet touched the floor the heavy cabinet was falling. I braced my body against it, pushing it back. Bottles and jars rained down from above. At the approach of my father's footsteps I fled upstairs and hid under a bed, far back in a corner where no one could reach me.

My curiosity was so compelling that I soon found myself familiar with the outside of the house as well as the inside. Although I was warned not to wander out of our back yard, I furtively extended my range until I knew all of the landmarks on our side of Sunnyland Street. I kept on the sidewalk, sensing when I was straying close to the curb by feeling a slight slant of the pavement and a crack between it and the major part of the sidewalk. I could tell my direction by the smell of trees, grass, and flowers. I learned to identify individual homes by the shapes of the terraces and hedges. I measured distances by following the edges of lawns with my foot. If I happened to be in a vacant lot I learned how to know my approximate position by the slant or rise of the ground, the tussocks of grass, the texture of shrubbery.

I was fond of going into one abandoned lot where there was an old mulberry tree in a corner. I would climb into its low-hanging branches, perch myself in a crotch between two boughs and sit for hours. This tree occupied most of my time in the out-of-doors. In spring it was covered with rough green berries, which I liked to rub between my fingers; in autumn, if any berries were left on the higher branches, I found them soft and sweet and full of juice. Sometimes, during the winter months when the air was crisp, I would find my way through the desolate garden, along the rough path leading to the alley, and thence to the old tree—just to see if it was still there.

Because of a strong inclination to use my hands to "look" at everything, I was prone to severe burns, bruises, and imbedded splinters of wood. As I became aware that my injuries caused ill-humor in the family, I learned to conceal them, hiding away until the pain had subsided. However, it was not always possible; I was often burned because I had been dipping my fingers into the pots and pans on the stove, or building fires in the garden.

My obsession with fire is difficult to explain. I would frequently secrete matches that I had stolen from the kitchen, gather bits of paper and wood and set them aflame in a nest of rocks. I would hold my hands above the blaze, feeling the heat flickering uneasily in the slightest wind. I could not see the fire, could not know the lure of its light, but it seemed to me a living thing. I was enchanted with the strange, acrid odors of burning things. Of course I was strictly forbidden to play with fire, but the urge to light small bonfires secretly and to sit by them as they gradually died into hot ashes was overwhelming.

My speech began to deteriorate soon after I was stricken with meningitis. With my small amount of residual hearing it was impossible for me to hear myself speak. As time passed, others spoke to me less frequently, since it was a bother to speak inches away from my ear and to repeat frequently what one said. At first my parents were unaware that I could not hear my own voice and asked me why I did not enunciate more clearly. Not being able to understand my predicament with regard to speech, or the reactions of the people around me, I withdrew more and more into my own shell.

To this day I cannot hear the sound of my voice and I have

no true concept of its character; but I would give a great deal to push aside the barrier and hear myself speak for only a few minutes.

While I still retained a remnant of hearing I was fascinated by loud noises. I was in the habit of playing records on our old phonograph, standing close to the speaker, my hand cupped behind my ear to catch the sounds. Of course I was not able to distinguish pitch or tone, or those delicate shadings of the chromatic scale which are essential for true appreciation of music; but I was captivated by the beat and rhythm of the melodies.

Curiously enough, my preoccupation with sounds continued even after I had lost my hearing entirely. I would sometimes run the bow across my sister's violin, merely to feel the variety of vibrations it would produce. I asked for harmonicas, horns, or drums for Christmas because I found pleasure in the sensations they produced through my fingertips.

I was aware of the characteristics of the various members of my family by running my hands over them. I had four sisters and a brother. My father worked in a Pittsburgh steel mill and each day when he came home, and Mother was still busy preparing the evening meal, I would sit on his lap and listen to him whistle. It sounded to me as though he always whistled the same tune.

Sometimes when he was free for a day he would go into the cellar to build small things for me. He made houses, bridges, and churches, all with the same care. There was skill in his short, strong fingers and I would sit nearby to wait until he finished the bench or cabinet he made from old wooden boxes. From the stray bits that dropped as his saw sang through the boards I would try to contrive little things of my own. But always I failed.

23

Bill, my brother, was almost a phantom to me. I was aware of his presence only at meals. After school he sold magazines or played tennis with his friends, or else he simply disappeared for hours on end without telling anyone where he went.

My sister Ruth was the nearest in age to me. We were continually teasing one another. Ruth had a club room for her small friends in our garage. I was curious about this place but I was never invited to visit it. Ruth kept the keys to the padlock and the window was always tightly closed. But one day I discovered that the latch of the window could be easily opened with one of my father's chisels; thereafter I frequently slipped through the window when Ruth was away, and wandered about the room, sniffing at empty perfume bottles and fingering castoff draperies and costumes. This started a feud between Ruth and me which lasted as long as the club existed.

Often we had races through the house, skidding on rugs and dashing up the stairs. I was able to follow Ruth with surprising efficiency. Once, however, I chased her into the bathroom and lost her. I closed the door and searched everywhere—in the bathtub, in the corners, behind the washstand. Just as I was about to give up hope of catching Ruth, I reached my hands out and felt her perched inside the washstand. I promptly turned the cold water on.

During those early years my mother was the closest person in the world to me. She was a plump little woman, who walked with a slight strut. Immaculate to the point of severity, she could not bear even a spot of dust or a crumb on the floor. She was especially meticulous about her garden, intolerant of any weeds in her beds of cockscombs, Chinese lanterns, bachelor's-buttons.

Mother was my teacher. I would sit for hours at her feet,

asking all the questions a small child can plague one with. She would read prayers and stories from the Bible slowly and distinctly into my ear. One day I asked, "Mommy, can I touch God?"

I felt her soft reply. "Yes, Bobby, you can touch God. If you reach out for Him, my darling, you will find Him at your fingertips, waiting to lead you safely through the darkness."

God at my fingertips—so immediate, as that? I was astonished. That night as I lay huddled under blankets, trying as usual to subdue my fear of the dark, I wondered about this strange answer of my mother's. The problem remained unsolved as I drifted into sleep.

2

Exactly one year and a month after my siege of cerebral spinal meningitis, my father introduced me to the Western Pennsylvania School for the Blind in Pittsburgh. I recall that morning in August soon after my sixth birthday with particular vividness because it was one of the rare times I was taken to "town" and enjoyed a trolley ride.

When we were ushered into the office of Mr. Joice, the superintendent, my father indicated to me that he desired to speak with him. I sat down, tracing the patterns on my chair, unaware of the conversation that was taking place. I had no inkling why we were there, except that my father had some sort of business to discuss with this man.

Within a few weeks we returned to the school. This time I was taken to the kindergarten, a building which was semi-isolated from the main school, having its own playground for the smaller children. That morning just before we left home my mother had told me I was going to school, like my brother and sisters. I felt a sense of jubilation at the thought that I was about to begin learning all sorts of new things, even though I hadn't the slightest understanding of what this might entail.

I was puzzled to find my father carrying a small suitcase. I asked him several times what was in it, but he refrained from answering. When we arrived at the school and I had been introduced to Miss Sprankle, the boys' matron, he took me up to the dormitory on the second floor and showed me my room, which consisted of a small bed, a locker, and a chair. Still it did not dawn upon me that these circumstances were of any immediate importance. When the time came for my father to leave he told me he would return soon. I believed him. I permitted myself to be led into the school-room by one of the teachers, where I spent the afternoon playing with toys.

But in the late afternoon, when all the other children had gone out into the playground, I began to wonder why my father hadn't come yet. I stood beside a large swing at the back of the playroom, feeling unutterably lonely. None of the other children paid the slightest attention to me as I sat on the swing and pushed myself back and forth. This novelty soon wore off and I stood behind it, my feeling of misery mounting with every minute. Finally I began to cry—quietly at first, then with more vehemence.

Miss Sprankle took me by the hand and led me from the shade into the warm sunshine of the playground. I went submissively, still crying softly, "When is my daddy coming?"

I could scarcely eat supper that evening, when one of the older children led me upstairs to my room. I undressed in a storm of tears, and, climbing into my cot, drifted into sleep, still goaded by the agony of being left alone in this unfamiliar place. That night I dreamed of my father. I saw him as I had known him when I had sight—tall, broad-shouldered, dressed in a brown suit, his hat perched jauntily on his head, with that warm smile that had always been so characteristic of him. This dream, repeated several times during the following weeks, retained such vividness that I have never forgotten it.

It developed that I was to stay at school Mondays through Fridays; my father would fetch me home for weekends.

For the first few weeks of my stay I was bewildered by my new surroundings. Instead of the snug rooms of my home, I was confronted by spacious areas where for many paces my fingers were unable to contact walls or furniture. Instead of parents over whom I had run my fingers familiarly, there were strange men and women whose clothes had an unfamiliar texture, whose movements were unfamiliar. Even the glossy furniture felt different to my touch.

With the blissful ignorance that seems an inseparable part of early childhood, I was not aware that there was any difference between myself and other children. I did not realize that the other kindergarten pupils were only blind while I was blind and steadily losing my hearing, the only student in the school to be so handicapped.

I was not invited to play many games with the other boys. I spent most of my time alone, wandering about the grounds, familiarizing myself with everything my hands could grasp or my fingers could touch in this new world into which I had been thrust. For guidance I followed the edges of lawns, the contours of curbs and walls, with my foot as I had done along my own street. Several times I wandered down the front walk to the street below the school, not knowing that this was forbidden territory. On other occasions I would find myself in the teachers' tennis court, the school's basement, and other unlikely places. Often I was able to find my way back again, but sometimes I had to be rescued by the matrons or one of the teachers. It was impossible for me to understand why these grownups gripped me so emphatically upon finding me or why they had such incisive voices when they tried to render explanations which were never coherent to me. And because of my limited understanding, I was incapable of explaining anything to myself.

Once, discovering a rock garden to the rear of the kindergarten, I explored the different plants, feeling their leaves and stems. While I was doing this I happened to stumble over a rock and tumble into a small fish pool whose presence I hadn't suspected. Fortunately I was able to recover my footing quickly and was soaked only up to my elbows. On another occasion, wandering over the girls' playground, I found myself surrounded by a group of little females who began to shout in what to me was a wordless singsong. Though I couldn't understand its meaning, I sensed there was a raucous quality that was meant to disturb me. I began to run as fast as I could, following the curbstone that hemmed in the lawn. As I fled, giggles rushed after me.

Gradually I got to know the different matrons and teachers of the kindergarten. There were two matrons. Miss Sprankle, the boys' matron, was elderly; her body was hard and bony. Whenever she spoke to me she sounded like a cat purring and when she became angry her voice rose to a screech. Miss Bloomer was the girls' matron. But when Miss Sprankle had a day off Miss Bloomer would replace her. I remember one day in early spring when Miss Bloomer decided to take me for a walk through the grounds. Timidly, for I was in great fear of her stern disposition, I permitted her to take my hand and lead me about, listening while she described the flowers and the games the other children were playing. When we came to a bed of daisies along the tennis court she told the boys playing there how to make daisy chains. And all the while she spoke, she held my hand. I have never forgotten that awesome walk. It seemed to stretch into hours.

I was continually getting into mischief. One day another boy suggested that we chase one another down the slippery tiled hall that led from the boys' playroom to the girls' side of the building. As I ran after him into the washroom, he suddenly closed the door behind him and my head struck a pane of frosted glass. There was the sound of splintering and cracking as the glass fell to the floor. Elizabeth, an attendant, came rushing over to me. I began to babble excited excuses, but Elizabeth, seeing the blood trickling down my forehead, carried me into the washroom. She paid no attention to anything I said as she bathed my cut. Then Miss Sprankle arrived. To my astonishment, she didn't punish me for my misbehavior.

"Poor little boy," Elizabeth crooned, "he is quite stunned. We'd better put him to bed for a while."

They carried me to the dormitory and laid me down. I was afraid I would miss supper and I asked if I would soon be allowed to get up. But all they said was, "Lie still and be quiet." I fell asleep and didn't awaken until the following morning.

My first kindergarten teacher—Mary Catherine Clare—was one of the most charming people I have ever known. The children loved to listen to her tales of fairies and giants, and of bad little children who became good again. Every afternoon our class began with an hour of singing. Miss Clare would sit at the piano and describe the adventures of a mountain lion in music. All the children would sit in a circle about the big schoolroom and sing. Our songs were simple ones, usually little poems Miss Clare set to music. I can still hear the rhythmic, childish voices:

> "Postman, postman, bring me a letter,
> Postman, postman, postman, do.
> One for the girls and one for the boys,
> One for me and one for you."

But at times I could barely understand the stories Miss Clare told us. My remnant of hearing often took on the artificial quality of a cheap phonograph. At such times I would squirm in my chair, growing more and more restive as the story wore on, pleading with Miss Clare to "talk louder." But she would protest that she was already using all her "wind" to reach me. Even on days when my hearing seemed at its best I missed a great many words. Yet here and there I was able to grasp bare essentials that provided the gist of a narrative.

During my first weeks in kindergarten I became acquainted with the hearing aid. I disliked it because I couldn't hear with it. The voices of the teachers sounded blurred and artificial, and I wanted to tear the tight, gripping earphone from my head. Finally, when the teachers noticed the failure of the instrument to help me, they gave up the enterprise and I returned to a happy frame of mind.

I looked forward eagerly to my first Christmas party in school. Each child was allowed to select from a list of wonderful things one toy he especially desired. We made our choice weeks in advance. When the great day arrived the kindergarten children marched over to the large main building for the celebration. There we waited in the auditorium for Father Santa to arrive with his gifts. Unable to hear the entertainment, I sat quietly in my chair, drifting into sleep. Now and then I would arouse myself and whisper to a nearby companion, "Is it time yet?" And when Santa finally came I shared in the general excitement.

Several weeks after I entered kindergarten Miss Clare taught me my first lessons in reading Braille. Braille is a series of cells with dots punched through heavy paper and raised so that they can be felt by the fingertips. I was first taught Braille through the use of zinc plates and peg boards. The zinc plates were embossed with Braille letters, which, after arduous practice, I learned to recognize with my fingers. It took me a number of weeks to recognize the first ten letters of the alphabet and to judge the distance between them. I was slower to assimilate Braille than the other students; my sense of touch had not yet been developed fully. Whenever I made a blunder Miss Clare, a stickler for perfection, would press my fingers down on the zinc dots or peg points with a violent gesture until I squirmed with pain. I kept on practicing until the tip of my forefinger grew numb and the skin was worn through; from time to time I would rub it on my sleeve to restore the circulation. Learning how to write in Braille was even more difficult than reading it. Our Braille slates consisted of two plates fastened together at one end by a hinge, with four lines of cells and vertical indentations for the placement of a stylus point. I was in the habit of making mistakes and then trying to erase them by rubbing out the dots. This left a noticeable flaw in the paper, which irritated Miss Clare no end. She would give a high-pitched moan, take my hand, and force her fingernails deep into my fingertips to indicate that she did not wish me to do any more erasing.

Such incidents failed to efface my enthusiasm for Miss Clare. I believe that all of us loved her for her genuine affection for us.

One morning when the kindergarten year was drawing to

a close I awoke and found my chest covered with a rash. When I rushed to Miss Sprankle and asked her what was wrong with me she told me I had measles. I was put to bed and became the last pupil to go home for the summer. During my confinement Miss Clare helped me while away the tedium by writing me a number of stories in Braille. In one she described an elephant who flopped mud all over an ant. In another she wrote about a shepherd dog and a little boy. In still another she told me about a good dog and a mean old bossy cow whom the dog helped to become a lady.

I dictated several letters for my parents to Miss Clare on her typewriter. I took an impish delight in giving the typewriter a sudden push and causing Miss Clare to make errors. Following is one such letter, which the family has preserved.

Dear Father and Mother:

I hope you are not worried about my eyes any more, because they are not harmed. This kind of measles doesn't hurt the eyes at all. I received your nice letter on Tuesday morning and it made me very happy. I hope to be home on Saturday of this week. Tell Aunt Nettie I thank her for the pretty birthday card. Oh boy! Was I glad to hear I am going to get a new cowboy suit. I know just how much fun I am going to have when I wear it. I can hardly wait till I find out what the other surprises are going to be, but I know they are going to be just fine and I can hardly wait to get home. I think it will be lots of fun to ride a pony in the park and I am going to make him go fast too.

Did you see any robins in our yard this week? We have a great many birds around here. The other day a baby bird flew in through the window and Miss Sprankle caught it and let us touch it. It was black and gray and it was just a tiny baby bird. There was a hole in the wall on the girls' side and a wee bird fell into it and Miss Sprankle picked it up and put it out where its mother would find it.

I am going to do a lot of work for you this summer, dust down the stairs every morning, throw the clothes down the chute, and do everything you want me to do. Did Ruthy stop school yet? I hope the birds do not bite our cherries. I hope that you are all well and that none of you has the measles.

Your loving little boy,
Bobby

I did not meet Miss Clare again until five years after I left kindergarten. Then one day during my fifth-grade term I was in the map room with the rest of my geography class, wandering aimlessly about while the others studied the large relief maps of various countries. I had already lost my hearing completely and it was impossible for me to follow the descriptions the teacher was giving to the others. My teacher came over to me and indicated that there was someone who would like to see me. As soon as I was led to the visitor I sensed it was Miss Clare. I cannot explain how I was able to recognize her. But something stirred my memory. I was astonished when she groped with her fingers to find mine. Then the truth flashed on me. *Miss Clare was as blind as I was.* She had had partial vision when I was in kindergarten. But during the ensuing years she had lost her remaining sight. "Bobby," her lips whispered as I read them with my fingers, "Now I know what it is to be sightless."

I ran my fingers eagerly over her. She was now past seventy. But she was the same lovable Miss Clare, with the same long slender neck, the silky hair worn in a bun at the back of it. Within a year she passed away and with her went a bit of my heart.

33

3

It was during the summer following my graduation from the fourth grade that the event so fearfully anticipated by the doctors took place. The remaining hearing in my right ear came to an end. One afternoon I was sitting with my mother in the parlor, playing a game at her feet. Suddenly I looked up and asked her a question. I could not hear her answer and I bent nearer until I felt her breath directly on my ear. Still I heard no reply. My father came over to speak to me. Both my parents shouted something I could not understand. Then we realized that I was completely deaf.

Strangely, I was not frightened. Perhaps I was not yet old enough to understand how serious this additional handicap was, or perhaps I had already lost my sense of hearing to such an extent that the complete silence did not bother me.

For weeks I lost all but the most elementary means of communication with my family. I sat quietly or played by myself in a corner. Whenever I wanted to communicate with my mother I would put my hand on her chin and ask what I wanted to know and she would shake her head "yes" or "no" in answer. I would place my hand on my father's face to learn whether he was pleased with anything I did.

On rare occasions my sister Grace volunteered to take me to the park; and while I slid or swung she would sit on the grass, surrounded by boys who never paid the slightest attention to me.

With the arrival of the fall the problem of resuming my studies seemed insuperable. And yet I had no desire to sit home, sealed off in darkness.

Groping about for some means by which I could communicate more extensively with Mother, one morning I had an inspiration. I put a pencil in Mother's hand.

"Mommy, teach me to make the letters of the alphabet."

Mother traced a large letter A on the side of the kitchen stove and then guided my hand as I drew it. She followed this with the letter B, and so on. I painstakingly traced the letters of the alphabet, practicing until I learned each character thoroughly. When I had mastered all twenty-six letters I had my mother trace them in my hand; but the point of the pencil was too sharp and I insisted that she use her fingers. Thereafter I communicated with my family in this makeshift fashion.

Four months after I lost my hearing my parents, after consulting with educational authorities, decided to send me back to the Western Pennsylvania School for the Blind. Although I was the only deaf-blind student enrolled, and the teachers were not trained to deal with my problem, they prepared to do what they could.

One morning shortly after my re-entrance I was called into the office of Mr. Joice, the superintendent. Without any preliminary explanation, he began to wriggle his fingers in the palm of my hand. He was introducing me to the manual alphabet for the deaf. This alphabet is a system of finger and knuckle positions of the hand, each position representing a given letter of the alphabet. Mr. Joice began by running my hands over the Braille alphabet, letter by letter, and transposing each into the corresponding letter in the manual alphabet. He had me repeat the procedure after him, indicating for me to form each letter as he formed it. We practiced this for an hour; then I was dismissed.

I had not dreamed that such a means of communication existed. Upon my return to the classroom I sat at my desk trying to recall the various positions of the hand in making the letters. Miss Magee, my teacher, came over and "talked" into my hand. We practiced together at a number of sessions.

"You're getting along fine, Bobby." Miss Magee would pat me on the head. "Soon you will be able to talk like a veteran."

Several of the boys became curious about this new method of "talking" and they practiced the alphabet so that they could communicate with me. But when they had talked a few times and their curiosity was appeased they quit using it and resumed their old practice of ignoring me. I was puzzled by their withdrawal. I couldn't understand why the happiness of conversation had been snatched from me. Resentfully I spelled into Miss Magee's hand, "Why have you asked me to learn the alphabet when none of the boys are interested in using it with me?"

To this Miss Magee had no answer. Her fingers remained silent.

My total loss of hearing greatly increased the difficulties of daily living. There were times when I felt as though I were groping about in infinite space with nothing to protect my balance. With the occurrence of deafness I had to re-discipline myself in the control of my facial features and each of my body muscles; it was necessary to perform even the simplest of physical operations with more deliberateness. Now when I peeled the skin off an orange, or cut a slice of bread in a cautious, sawing motion, checking with my left hand to provide that the knife did not slant too much either way, I was conscious of undertaking these actions in a world stripped of one more dimension.

More than ever my fingers were critically important to me. The nerves of my face and feet as well as my hands provided me with information. I detected changes in the weather by the weight of the air on my face. The air at night is heavier than during the day and the fragrance of the night world is more clearly defined to my nostrils. If I had not been violating the conventional time table, I would have much preferred to do my living in the evening and sleep all day. When the earth is hushed, senses are much more alive. The night winds are the master music makers of the skies.

Not only the night but every change in climate moved me. Once, when there had been a furious thunderstorm and a great evergreen tree on the grounds of the school was struck by lightning, with part of its limbs left standing petrified above the cleavage of wreckage, I went around for several days in a state of depression.

My interest in people was not diminished by deafness. Touch increasingly became my criterion for judging appearances. I judged whether the person before me was plain or attractive by the size and shape of his cheeks, the formation of his head and lips, the texture of his hair. In shaking hands, I determined by the height of the forearm whether a person was short, medium, or tall. I estimated by the handclasp whether he had a gentle, sympathetic or an aggressive personality. There is so much a handshake reveals about human character—there is a brave handclasp, a weary touch, a sly touch, a clasp full of profound depression.

Gradually I became acclimated to the routine of the Western Pennsylvania School for the Blind. I depended upon vibrations and smells to give me an inkling of the passage of time. Most of the floors in the classrooms were wooden. When I felt the clamor of rising bodies, the impact of arms and legs striking against my desk (or when I sensed the odor of passing humans), I knew it was time to change classes. Whenever the floor happened to be made of stone I found it more difficult to determine whether a class was over. Often I would touch a fellow student to make certain he was still there, or I would push my book along my desk until it touched another pupil's body.

At school I continued to take the same studies as the hearing students, with the exception of music. My woodwork class was an illustration of tedious study. Our teacher, James Schroeder, was a hunchback with an unpredictable disposition. He could be witty and cheerful one day and irascible the next. Few of the boys accomplished much of anything in Mr. Schroeder's shop—only those pupils who had extraordinary skill or enough sight to enable them to pursue their studies with reasonable efficiency.

Mr. Schroeder's shop smelled crisply of razor-sharp tools and newly cut birch and pine. Helping ourselves to a plank, we would smell the grain to determine what kind of wood we had selected and we would dig our fingernails into the surface to judge whether the wood was firm enough to take our hammering. On more than one occasion, in attempting to straighten a nail, I missed it altogether and mashed my fingers; great spurts of blood gushed out over the board and dripped over my shirt and pants. Once I was laid up in the infirmary for a week with broken knuckles and a swollen wrist.

I entered Mr. Schroeder's class just before losing my hearing and I continued with my woodwork after I was unable to hear his voice. Yet even today there are times when that sardonic voice rings in my memory. "Ah, sonny, what are you doing wrong? What are you doing wrong?" This was the manner in which he addressed us as he examined our pitiful efforts to drive nails cleanly into boards and bevel the end of planed surfaces.

As the weeks, following my loss of hearing, lengthened into months, I came to terms with my world of silence. The silence was not a vacuum by any means. It had a personality, indeed several distinct personalities of its own. At times it was a dead-weight silence that pressed down on me—a silence so oppressive that on the warmest days of the year I would be seized by shivers—and yet at other times it was a tender yielding silence that seemed to tremble with the terrible desire to speak. Time and again voices lurked on the borders of my existence, and I was convinced that if I bent my ear and subdued the beating of my heart I would be able to hear them, but always, when I strained for the effort, they would elude me.

The problems I faced socially became more acute as time passed. One difficulty that related directly to my loss of hearing was the deterioration of my speech. Unable to hear the sound of my voice, I gradually lost my feeling for the pitch and stresses that give speech its human character. One day as I was reciting an assignment, Miss Stavoe, one of my teachers, spelled into my hand, "Bobby, do you realize you are not pronouncing a single word clearly? We simply will have to do something about you."

By various means the teachers sought to bolster my speech. One method was to have me memorize lines of poetry. One Thanksgiving I learned with horror that I had been selected to recite a poem before the entire school. Miss Levy drilled me for weeks to articulate eight lines properly. My anxiety mounted with every passing hour. But when the occasion arrived, I mustered all my courage and began:

> "The world is full of gladness,
>   There are joys of many kinds,
>   There's a cure for every sadness,
>   That each living mortal finds.
>
> "And if anybody asks you,
>   Just tell them what I say,

Tell them that you're thankful,
For Thanksgiving Day."

When the program was over I asked my parents anxiously, "Did I speak clearly enough?"

My mother's fingers hesitated. "Well, Bobby, you didn't speak so that we could hear *every* word."

The deterioration of my speech brought about a disintegration of my relations with the other boys at school. There were various circumstances that provoked their scorn. Many of the boys had partial vision; all of them had hearing. My habit of feeling and smelling everything irritated them. They gave me the nickname "Smearcase." Before I went deaf I would hear the high-pitched cries when I approached. "Let's go away, fellows. Smearcase is here!" Most of the time I couldn't even make out the words, but the cry was so often repeated with such intensity that I always recognized it.

One of the favorite pastimes of the boys was to creep up on me, give me a sudden shove, and run as I was sent sprawling. Most of the time I would get to my feet without a word and walk away. But sometimes my anger got the best of me, and I would make quick dashes after my tormentors. Usually this ended in my running into a wall.

The other boys, I discovered, would tolerate my presence only when I had candy in my pocket. I was one of the lucky ones who went home during weekends and on Monday mornings I would return to school well supplied with fruit, candies, and cookies. In the class of older boys there were several fellows who were especially unkind to me. However, one day, when they discovered that I had several packages of chewing gum in my pockets, they made friendly overtures.

"Let's go for a walk," George spelled into my hand.

"I don't want to walk."

"Oh, come on. Just for a little while. We can have a lot of fun together."

Not wishing to antagonize these boys who were larger than myself, I consented. George took my arm and Blakely walked on the other side of me. We strolled up and down the hall for a few turns. Then George tripped me and I fell. When I picked myself up I found them groping along the floor.

"What are you looking for?"

"Oh, nothing," said George. "I think I dropped something."

They left me after a while. Later when I searched my pockets for my chewing gum I discovered that the packages had vanished. George and Blakely had done a thorough job.

Holding onto my goodies became a positive obsession with me. Frequently when I came into class on Mondays with pockets stuffed, the matron would ask me to give her the sweets for safekeeping.

One day, tortured by dark suspicions, I sat down and typed out a letter to the superintendent, Mr. Joice:

Dear Mr. Joice:

Mrs. Smith takes away my fruit and says that you told her to. Would you mind giving me a reason? You see I don't trust her because she eats some of the boys' fruit and gives the rest away and the owner gets only a tiny bit of it. She collected a whole bag last week and she said that she was going to give the nuts to the squirrel. But the boys say that *she* is the squirrel and I agree. I have told my parents before that I did not like to have her take away my fruit since I am old enough to take care of it myself. If she keeps on taking it, I will be fearfully angry.

Bobby Smithdas

The older boys in school had a hobby of baiting the smaller fellows into fist fights. For a long time a group of them had their eye on me, plotting how they could trick me into a brawl. Finally they seized upon Johnny, a boy my own age with Negro and Indian blood, and they worked on him to lure me into a scrap. I knew that Johnny had partial vision and I was reluctant to accept the challenge. However, under his persistent insults I was forced to yield. My pride would not let me slink away.

The match took place in the boys' sitting room. Although fights were strictly forbidden, a crowd herded in here surreptitiously and egged us on. There was a round table screwed down to the floor in the center of the room. My adversary adopted hit-and-run tactics, exploiting my inability to see him. He punched me and raced around the table as I chased him to retaliate. Every now and then he would suddenly stop, lean across the table, and deliver quick short jabs that caught me flush on the jaw. My efforts to close in on him were futile. I made aimless dashes about the room, only to have him dodge and appear from another direction. Suddenly he caught me a smashing blow on the nose. I felt a numbing sensation, and a rivulet of warm blood running down my chin. My throat tightened and my veins throbbed with hot insensate anger. Every last inhibition vanished. My thoughts concentrated with a terrible intensity on the one important objective—to retaliate, to deal him, blow by blow, the pain he had inflicted on me. I lunged across the room and closed in on him. Grabbing him in a bear hug, I began to pummel him, my arms working like trip hammers. I felt him grow limp.

Presently hands seized me, separated me from my quarry, dragged me to a corner of the room. The atmosphere was tremulous. Several older boys had hurriedly intervened and broken up the fight before I could do any further damage.

I slipped out of the room, made my way to the washroom, placing my bleeding nose under the faucet. Then, aware that the boys were leaving for the afternoon class, I walked across the campus, feeling resentful.

One morning shortly afterward Miss Stavoe, my teacher, took me aside and spoke into my hand. "Bobby, you are falling behind badly in your speech. And you are not to blame. We just don't have the time or the means here for dealing with you properly. My boy, for the sake of your future, you should be sent somewhere else where you can get the proper individual instruction."

I walked away embarrassed, not fully understanding what Miss Stavoe meant, convinced that somehow I had failed her and she was rebuking me.

One night, as I tossed in my bed unable to sleep, I recalled a tragedy that had taken place the previous autumn when I still had hearing and that now served to place my own predicament in a proper perspective.

One Friday morning my brother Bill had called for me at school to take me home. Usually my father came for me in the evening, and I had been surprised to find Bill waiting in the reception room.

"Hurry and get your suitcase, Bobby," he shouted into my ear. " 'Becksrun' Grandma is dead."

"Becksrun" Grandma was my maternal grandmother—a wonderful woman. She loved flowers and all growing things and was steadfast in her utter faith in God. Whenever my parents had taken me to visit her and my grandfather in their old house on the hill I would run my fingers over the embroidered cap that covered her hair, and feel her hands for the nuts and pennies she usually saved for me.

I had never been to a funeral before, and I was frightened when, upon returning home, I was taken into the large room where her body lay and told to kneel beside the coffin. The scent of roses and lilies filled the warm air almost to the point of suffocation. After I had said a short prayer my father placed my fingers on my grandmother's hands, folded quietly on her breast. They were cold and stiff to my touch. I shivered.

Sadness is a heavy thing and I was glad to leave that flower-filled room, with the cold, stiff fingers, in which I had experienced a silence even more profound than the living silence of my own world.

And now as I lay in my bed, recalling this first experience with death, I felt curiously at peace. My mother had assured me that God had reached down for "Becksrun" Grandma in the depths of her stillness and had led her into the living world. Had He not promised that the dead would rise again? But if He had accomplished this for "Becksrun" Grandma, how could I have any doubt that He would reach out for me in my much less overwhelming isolation? Yes, God was at my fingertips.

Quietly I fell asleep.

Chapter II

"The Journey of a Thousand Miles..."

MIDWAY in the fifth grade my educational career underwent
a change. Late one afternoon just before supper I was summoned to Mr. Joice's office. Mr. Joice seemed to be in excellent humor. He gripped my hand in a friendly fashion and
indicated that I should be seated. Two men entered the
room. I was aware of their presence by the odor of cigarette
smoke mingled with a flowery smell of after-shave lotion and
talcum powder. Mr. Joice introduced me to the strangers and
I mumbled "hello." In a few moments Miss Hoof, my
teacher, appeared and spelled out in my hand a letter written
by her and my classmates. I was astounded to discover it was
a farewell letter to me. Lacking the facilities to provide me
with the specialized training I needed, the school authorities
had made arrangements to send me on a scholarship to Perkins institute in Watertown, Massachusetts.

I was later to learn that Perkins was world famous as a
school for educating blind and deaf-blind children. It had
been founded in 1832 by Dr. Samuel Gridley Howe, a Bos-

45

ton surgeon, who from all accounts had combined the humanitarianism of a Grenfell with the dash of Byron. Indeed, after graduating from Brown University at the age of twenty, he dashed off—like Byron—to aid the Greeks as an army physician in their struggle to overthrow the Turks, who had ruled despotically for over four hundred years. When the Greeks had attained their independence he returned to America. He became interested in the hardships of the blind and, with the aid of a grant from the Massachusetts state legislature, opened a pioneer school for the blind in Boston. Thomas Handasyd Perkins, a wealthy Boston merchant, donated his home, and the school assumed his name. Howe searched the state, going into obscure towns and farm areas, and brought back six blind children for his first class.

Howe's experiments were of fundamental importance. Until the seventeenth century the blind and deaf-blind of the world had been social pariahs. Blind babies had been strangled by the Greeks, tossed into the Tiber by the Romans instead of being permitted to grow up and become "liabilities" to the community. In China blind girls were sold by their parents into prostitution. In medieval times the blind roamed the streets as beggars with tin cups, and in modern times the deaf-blind were clapped away in asylums for the insane.

This information about Dr. Howe and Perkins I learned over the years after I had taken up residence at the school. Naturally when the morning came for me to say good-by to my mother and leave with my father on the train for Boston, I hadn't the foggiest notion of what lay ahead for me. Boston seemed like a distant corner of the earth. I could sense my mother's mounting excitement as we packed my things and made final preparations. "Remember, Bobby," she scrawled in the palm of my hand. "Work hard and keep out of trouble. And above all, don't fight with the other boys. You will never have a chance like this again."

Father and I were scheduled to leave Pittsburgh on an evening train. It was a wintry night with sharp cold that had a faint, musty odor about it. I kissed my mother good-by, holding her very close. It would be June before I saw her again. Home seemed suddenly so warm and snug and desirable. I fought hard against the temptation of tears.

The train was crowded with soldiers and sailors and other passengers. People were sitting on suitcases or standing in the aisles; it was wartime, and all the trains were filled to capacity. But by the middle of the night, after we had left Harrisburg, the coach became less encumbered with human beings. Father and I slept bolt upright on the hard seats, our heads drooping uncomfortably.

Toward morning the train stopped. Gradually the heat of the coach faded away and a cold, incisive chill set in. The train had stalled, my father told me, and no one knew how long we would be stranded on the tracks. An hour passed; then we began to move again. It was a common experience that thousands encountered during the war years when troops and supplies were being moved all over the country, but we were so chilled that it was impossible for us to sleep again, despite our heavy overcoats. We stayed awake until the train reached Boston in the early morning, both of us silent and miserable. Father kept looking out of the windows; I dug my hands into my pockets, hunched my shoulders deep into my collar, and kept thinking how wonderful it would be to have breakfast at home with my mother.

Finally the train pulled into South Station. Though I was weary, I was glad to leave the cramped, dusty coach, happy to be walking again in the cool sunlight, with a bracing wind fanning my cheeks. The excitement I had known the night before, which had been dampened by the long journey, returned with a sudden rush.

Father suggested breakfast.

"I'm not hungry, Dad."

"We'll have to eat anyway. We still have time—and it's a long way to the school yet."

We picked our way through the early-morning throngs near the station and found a small lunchroom. Father ordered sugared ham and scrambled eggs for me, pressing the silverware into my hand. "You won't have another meal until we reach the school."

When we left the lunchroom father hailed a taxi and we started the drive to Watertown. Neither of us spoke as we rode through the streets of Boston and into the suburbs. Father was evidently tired after the previous night, and I was too absorbed with my own thoughts to ask my usual questions about the scenery we were passing.

Morning classes had already begun when we finally stood in the lobby of the Howe Building at Perkins. I felt my Braille watch; it was nine-thirty. We were directed to the office of Miss Inez Hall, who headed the department for the deaf-blind. It was a cosy little room off the main corridor. As we entered the office we were greeted by a woman who took my hand and held it in a friendly way.

It was Miss Hall. "How are you, Bob?" She used the manual alphabet.

I was grateful when she added, "Please sit down. I want to talk to your father."

However, as time passed I grew restive. Having to sit in silence until someone chooses to communicate with you is difficult, particularly when you are tense with curiosity about what is going on. I passed my hand over the wood of the chair on which I was confined, became aware of a bookcase filled with books of assorted sizes, and papers and boxes and an iron radiator of unappealing symmetry behind me. Finally when I reached a point of acute nervous tension Miss Hall took my hand and said, "It is nearly time for your dinner, Bob. Your father will go with you to your cottage to see your room, then you can come back, and we will have a little chat of our own."

Miss Hall opened the door and directed my hand to a man who must have been waiting in the small study room nearby. He shook it vigorously.

"This is Henry," Miss Hall said. "He will introduce you to Ralph Feliciano, who will be your attendant. Ralph will accompany you whenever you leave the cottage, to your classes and on strolls through the campus. It is a rule of the school that every deaf-blind pupil must have a seeing attendant."

Henry guided my father and me out of the main building, along the campus and opened the door of Tompkins Cottage. He left us in the hallway, standing beside a small, rather ugly table, and went off to fetch Miss Harmening, the matron.

Miss Harmening soon appeared and put a large capacious hand, almost masculine in texture, into mine. Her grip was astonishingly firm. Some time later I learned that she had been reared on a Dakota farm where she had milked cows. She was proud of those "strong milking hands." She was an exceedingly virile woman with heavy square shoulders and a massive movement when she walked. I was to be continually confused by her abrupt bursts of humor.

Miss Harmening knew the manual alphabet for the deaf and she spelled into my hand with a slow, deliberate motion, inviting me to come into the dining room for lunch. I followed her and took my place at the table, running my fingers over the place mats, the cane-bottom chairs. Not a single detail escaped me. I tried to estimate what the other children around the table were doing. I tasted the roast beef cautiously, sampled the mashed turnips. I did not like their rough, bitter flavor, but I relished the hot crisp rolls with their tasty crust.

When the meal was over my father prepared to leave for home. Good-bys were said in Miss Hall's office. Dad talked to Miss Hall for a few moments, laughing and nodding in his most sociable vein. Presently I noted that his hat was in his hand. "Write home often, Bob. Don't let your mother worry about you."

It was Ralph Feliciano who showed me to my room at the upper end of the hall in Tompkins Cottage where I was to unpack my belongings. I stumbled as I climbed the spiral staircase, the first such staircase I had ever mounted. My room had only two beds, one for my attendant and one for myself, and a closet for each of us. I was delighted with the prospect of such privacy.

"There are four cottages on the campus," Ralph informed me by manual. "We all live in family groups. You'll like it fine here. Do you ice skate?"

I shook my head.

"Well, you'd better learn. We have skating on Dead Horse Pond. The boys call it that because a horse is said to have drowned there during Colonial times. The Indians used to camp around the pond and you can still pick up flint stones and arrowheads if you go digging around there. In the spring when the ice melts the boys go rowboating and swimming on the lake."

I expressed interest and indicated that he should go on.

"You'll surely like the apple orchard behind old Doc Farrell's house. Dr. Farrell's the director of the school. The boys sneak in there and hoist themselves up to steal the juiciest apples. They're supposed to keep off the grounds, but the attendants never squeal on them. We just stand by and take part of the loot."

I nodded sympathetically. The possibilities of Perkins quite overwhelmed me.

"By the way, Bob, I want you to meet Leonard Dowdy."

"Who is Leonard Dowdy?"

"Leonard is the other deaf-blind boy in the department. Henry is Leonard's attendant. I'm sure you'll get to know him well. He lives just down the hall."

I was tremendously curious about Leonard Dowdy. I had never met another deaf-blind person before.

The meeting took place that night immediately after supper.

Leonard came into my room with Henry. As soon as our mutual shyness wore off he proved to be a boy with irrepressible enthusiasm. Inviting me to run my hands over him, he entertained me with imitations of various animals. My hand caught the vigorous movements of a tiger, a bear, a pig, and barnyard fowl, complete with the waddling about and clucking.

Leonard spent the entire evening crawling about as a quadruped for my entertainment, and he punctuated his exhibitions with a stream of chatter which was interpreted into my hand by Henry, his attendant. Leonard was fourteen, two years younger than I was, when I arrived at Perkins. He was one of the three deaf-blind pupils at the school—the other two were girls. He had lost his sight and hearing at the age of twenty-one months from spinal meningitis. Leonard came to Perkins at five, and his sunny disposition had won everybody to him. Although he crawled about on all fours and couldn't speak a word, he was a naturally intelligent little fellow. Finding out that it was very painful for him to bump his head when proceeding forward blindly, he trained himself to crawl backward, preferring to bump his rump if need be. Within a year after his arrival he learned to speak and understand forty words and count to ten. Much as a dog is taught to perform tricks, Leonard was first taught to respond to commands. "Bow," ordered the teacher, or, "Get the rug out of the cupboard, put it on the floor, and sit on it." Leonard learned to comply alertly. Every night before going to bed, he was taught to kneel, join his hands, and say:

> I love Papa,
> I love Mama,
> I love God.
> Amen

At the time of my arrival Leonard had been at Perkins for nine years. He was able to hold conversations and express ideas within the range of his limited experience and knowledge.

In subsequent weeks Leonard was to become my closest friend. His enthusiasm was so insatiable that it acted as a tonic on me. He had been brought up in total innocence that he was different from other people and he enjoyed life with abandon. Indeed, his physical exuberance had the teachers constantly worried. One night he climbed out of the window of his room, hoisted himself to the roof and crawled along the ledge, singing in the darkness. The entire campus was thrown into consternation. While the teachers stood by, terrified, two night watchmen had to climb out onto the ledge and bring him down to safety.

Although Leonard was my junior, he had a brash assurance, and he airily overruled my opinions. He insisted upon having his way even in the most trivial matters, and if I crossed him, he would explode in a tantrum. However, his gaiety would always win me back to him.

Early in our acquaintance I noticed that Leonard walked with a curious, swaying gait, quite unlike anything I had ever experienced. I discovered that this was due to fallen arches in his feet, caused by his tendency to feel the ground with his entire foot. I found out also that he was extraordinarily sensitive to physical pain. This, however, did not prevent him from taking impish risks like the excursion on the roof.

Gradually, during my strolls with Ralph Feliciano, I became familiar with the grounds of Perkins; and, as the weeks passed, I became acquainted with its history. It had been a principle with the founders of Perkins that the unseeing and unhearing should live in an aesthetically inspiring environment, for beauty has its own channels of communication even when the senses are deficient.

Perkins' thirty-four acres overlooked the placid waters of the Charles River. Its classrooms and cottages were rambling brick buildings in Tudor Gothic style, covered with ivy. The bell tower of a chapel soared above the campus, providing a familiar landmark to Bostonians. Visitors saw it when they were several miles away. When spring arrived, only weeks after my entrance, I spent happy hours strolling amid the giant pines, the ancient oak and maple trees. When April opened its deep blue eyes the air was permeated with their old-fashioned perfumes. The old chestnut in front of Tompkins Cottage broke into blossom, its wonderfully flowering branches overhanging the low wall that ran along the campus. After a few weeks of bloom the blossoms fell, covering the ground with a muffled carpet. And when I walked along the flagstone paths of the herb garden my footsteps crushed the leaves of thyme and sorrel, sending up a curtain of tart, mingled fragrances that hung like a giant censer in the sunlit air.

In the autumn when the leaves were turning and there was a faint, acrid odor of burning so characteristic of the season, I delighted in the aroma of ripening grapes and apples. The vines in the grape arbor and the orchards had been planted by Dr. Allen, a former director of the school. There were quinces too, and behind the administration building in a grassy place I found pear trees growing.

During my first months at Perkins I grew especially fond of a magnolia tree in the director's garden. It was not a tall tree, but an impressive one. In springtime it would put forth drooping flowers, shaped like the mouthpieces of old-fashioned telephones, with long slender stamens at their hearts. I delighted in their long, filmy petals, the evasive sweetness hidden in their cups.

Just a few weeks after my arrival (before the wonders of spring unfolded) one of those unpredictable storms that occasionally whirl along the coast of New England burst over us, and an ancient gnarled oak fell across the school fence facing the Charles River. None of the teachers or students seemed to know exactly how long it had been standing there, but its great trunk bent the iron rods as it fell.

One morning Leonard Dowdy flew into one of his temper tantrums and, for punishment, he was sent out to cut cross sections from its hardy wood. Eager to share the exercise, I went along with Leonard and drew the crosscut sword with him. It was strenuous work. The blade cut into the heartwood inch by inch. It took us more than two hours to saw cleanly through the three-foot giant. Though the circle we cut was only six inches in thickness, it was so heavy we had to roll it to move it out of place.

When I arrived at Perkins there were over two hundred students attending the school, in classes ranging from kindergarten through high school. Surprising revelations about the place seemed unceasing. Only a few days after my arrival I had one of them. Joe Jablonske, who had been assigned to me as a student instructor, spelled into my hand facts about the history of Perkins. I had learned at the Pennsylvania School for the Blind about Helen Keller, but I had never dreamed that she had had a predecessor at Perkins.

"Bob, have you ever read anything about Laura Bridgman?" Mr. Jablonske asked.

"No? Who is she?"

"She was the first totally deaf-blind person who ever succeeded in getting an education."

"Well, I know about Bridgman Cottage on the Boys' Close."

"That was named after Laura. Let's go up to the library and get out some material on her. We may even be able to see her brain."

"What are you talking about?" I was convinced that Joe was being facetious. But Joe was evidently quite serious.

We left the classroom and took the nearby steps to the Blindiana Library. This library is one of the distinctive features of Perkins; it contains mementos, models, and samples dealing with every phase of work for the blind. It contains books and manuscripts pertaining to famous blind people and texts written upon the problems of blindness from the earliest writers of the Christian era to the present day.

I found that Joe had been right—the library had a plaster cast of Laura Bridgman's brain. But it was sealed in a glass case and I was unable to touch it. It is one of the treasures of the Perkins collection. Joe described it to me, and

I tried my best to visualize its exact proportions. There was also Laura's needlework on display, and I was disappointed that I was unable to finger this also. But Joe found me a small volume dealing with Laura's life. I took this to my room and plunged into it.

Laura was born to a New Hampshire farm couple in 1828; she lost her sight and hearing from scarlet fever before she was three. Dr. Samuel Howe, scouring the state for pupils to take back to his newly opened school, came upon the child when she was eight and persuaded her parents to let him take her to Perkins. The child not only was deaf and blind; she was unable to speak. Leading medical authorities had stated positively that no child so afflicted could be given an education. Howe was faced with a problem that had never before been solved—how to educate a deaf-blind person. "Her mind," he wrote to friends, "dwells in darkness and stillness as profound as that of a closed tomb at midnight."

Howe began an experiment that has become a classic in the history of education. He pasted on a fork, key, spoon and other articles in daily use the name of each in raised letters. He had Laura feel the object and the lettering until she was able to associate one with the other so skillfully that when the labels were detached from the objects, she was able to match them again. Next she learned to take the individual letters of each label and arrange them to form each name. Up to now the process was simply mechanical. But Howe reported in his description of the experiment, "As the truth began to flash upon her, her intellect began to work; she perceived that here was a way by which she could herself make up a sign of anything that was in her own mind and show it to another mind; and at once her countenance lighted up with a human expression; it was no longer a dog or parrot—it was an immortal spirit, eagerly seizing upon a new link of union with other spirits!"

Under Howe's guidance Laura explored the world of ideas, learned to write letters to her friends, to knit and sew. Although she never reached the level of mental achievement of Helen Keller, never went to college or even learned to speak, yet she was the first deaf-blind person to be restored, even if only partially, into the world of the living.

Dr. Howe loved Laura like a daughter, and she was passionately attached to him. In the words of Dickens, who met her, Dr. Howe "came next to the God she adored."

All this I learned that blustery February day as I sat in my room devouring the little volume. My excitement was immense. As my fingers passed over the print, my head swarmed with questions. I wondered how Laura had been able to thread a needle with her tongue; why she had frequently dreamed in sign language; how Dr. Howe had found the patience to educate her. What a pity there was so little information about such a marvelous story. I deplored the scanty volume in my hands. Were there no other facts one could get about Laura Bridgman? I tried to imagine Laura as she must have been as a young girl, wondering whether she had experienced the same cold sweat, the nagging fears that I had known and mastered only through self-control. Had she too been afraid of being lost in strange, unfamiliar places, of colliding with bruising objects in her path?

While Laura had never succeeded in learning to speak, Perkins within recent years had developed techniques that provided a deaf-blind individual with a method of articulation, assuming that he had the will and patience to persist in the practice required.

Miss Inez B. Hall, the head of the department for the

deaf-blind, gave me my first lesson in these techniques, a few days after my arrival.

"Bob, the first steps to take in getting you to articulate clearly will be to discontinue the use of the manual alphabet."

She paused. "I am going to teach you to hear me speak by reading the vibrations of my voice with your fingers. In learning to read me, you will develop the means for speaking clearly yourself."

Miss Hall placed my hand on her face in such a way that my thumb pressed against her lips, my index finger ran alongside of her throat just under the line of her jaw. I was completely mystified by the vibrations of her larynx as her lips moved slowly and deliberately, forming words against my thumb. But I was fascinated by the changing expressions of her face. Then, indicating for me to withdraw my thumb and fingers, she explained in my hand what she was trying to accomplish. "In reading speech, Bob, you will learn to think in terms of vibrations just as other people learn to think in terms of language."

Miss Hall put a chart before me, which contained in Braille all the basic sounds of speech. After I placed my finger over the transcription of "ah" and "oh," I placed my finger on Miss Hall's tongue and found that it lay soft and flat in her mouth. Then I placed my hand on her chest and felt the vibrations of sound when she pronounced the vowels. I investigated the sounds of the labial consonants by feeling the vibrations in her nose as her breath was drawn through it. When Miss Hall pronounced "ja," "jam," I felt a pronounced vibration on her chin bone. When she formed "p," "t," I detected a stoppage of her breath followed by a quick release of it. When Miss Hall pronounced "sh," I felt a short flow outwards of breath on the palm of my hand.

In this fashion I was initiated into the Tadoma method of lip reading—a method introduced at Perkins by Miss Alma Todd, who carried on researches with Miss Hall. The first lesson was a mere introduction to the study. Long, painstaking hours passing into weeks and months would be necessary to learn to read even the simplest sentences. That first afternoon Miss Hall spoke into my thumb and fingers for nearly an hour. I was not accustomed to hold my hand in such an unusual position and the muscles of my shoulder began to throb painfully. As the lessons continued, my muscles strengthened, my fingers grew less weary.

Miss Hall astonished me one morning by having me take off my shoes and socks, lie on my back, and raise my toes to her lips. I learned that this was one of the methods used to develop greater sensitivity to vocal vibrations. The vibrations I received from her speech were not received in the toes so much as in the balls of the feet.

Actually, despite my efforts, it was to be fifteen years before I was able to lecture naturally and with entire confidence to a room full of people.

However, much sooner than that I became skillful at speech reading—but only under certain conditions. I found, for instance, that I couldn't read lips outdoors in very cold weather, since the colder the fingers, the less receptive they are to vibrations. To this day, my success at lip reading varies with the individual. A New England or Midwestern accent is fairly easy to read, because it is close clipped; the Southern accent is much more difficult because it is soft and open. Women's voices are easier to read than men's because of their higher rate of vibration.

Regardless of my uncertain success, lip reading opened up

an entirely new world of communication to me. For the first time I was able to appreciate with my fingers the changing relationships of the voice and facial expression. I learned that anger, for instance, is a very generalized emotion; the voice becomes harsher and often rises in pitch; the mouth tightens; the head invariably thrusts forward; and the body becomes more rigid in posture. I found that people who are in an argumentative mood usually shake their heads slightly from side to side, and that they lean forward almost imperceptibly. But what intrigued me most was the action of smiling. I loved to watch people smile; loved to notice how their bodies lost tension, their cheeks rounded, and their whole attitude changed to one of pleasant relaxation. However, I also noted that some people laugh without mirth—without the swift release of tension that makes the whole body quiver a little with pleasure.

I noticed also that there are two distinct kinds of smiles: the smile that pulls the corners of the mouth upward, and the smile that turns them downward. Correspondingly, I discovered that those whose smiles curled upward at the corners were usually the happiest people to know. I was so enthralled with this idea that I experimented with myself. I spent several days smiling in each way, often contrasting the two methods so that I could compare them and their effects upon my own feelings. Turning the corners of my mouth downward inevitably made me feel restrained and a trifle forced; while turning the corners upward suffused me with a glowing sense of well-being.

Upon my arrival at Perkins I was given individual instruction in all my studies, something a deaf-blind student absolutely requires and something I was unable to obtain at my former school. By degrees I regained the confidence I had lost at the Pennsylvania School. The teachers made studying fun. Mr. Burke, who taught me commercial arithmetic, developed my powers at mental calculation by having me compute the batting averages of Stan Musial, Joe DiMaggio, and Ted Williams. I spent many an hour with him at this mathematical game.

Mr. Gibson, my science teacher, injected drama into his experiments. When I started to study fireless cookers he made a crude model of one out of grocery boxes and old newspapers and he brought baked beans and cooked wheat into the classroom. To prove how it would keep its heat, he deposited them overnight in his fireless cooker. The following morning they were still hot and I was given a dish to taste. Mr. Gibson never went halfway and so there was a pot of coffee and rolls to go with the dish. I ate three dishes of beans and consumed several rolls and cups of coffee. Mr. Gibson was staggered by my appetite.

Mr. Mabey, my handicraft instructor, was a kindly soul with boundless patience and old-fashioned courtesy. He had taught at Perkins for fifty-three years and under him I experienced the pleasure of making baskets. Stroking the weaves and feeling the undulating rhythm brought me excitement.

The teaching aids used by my instructors were decidedly helpful. In algebra, for instance, I learned to plot graphs on thick paper with raised lines stretched over balsa wood. The axes were marked with rubber bands stretched on either side of the board. I plotted the points that satisfied the equation by sticking pins into the balsa bed. Then I stretched a rubber band over these points, plotted the second equation in the same way. I marked down the co-ordinates where the points met with a stylus pencil. In geometry I gained a conception of triangles, squares, cubes, by modeling figures in plasticine. With the ends of my steel compass I perforated the paper to label my diagrams in Braille. In geography I made maps by rolling strips of plasticine into bays and peninsulas. Rivers were indicated by even thinner strips; and lakes by plasticine molded into circles or oblongs to approximate the actual shape given by the embossed map that served as a guide at my elbow. The plasticine was progressively graded for plains, plateaus and mountaintops. By pinching the plasticine, I raised up excellent mountains; white plasticine was used to represent peaks that were covered with snow all year round. I spread tin foil to make my rivers glisten properly. I represented cities with beads, deserts with sandpaper. The hilly regions of deserts were indicated by building up glue or gesso and sea sand.

The plasticine maps and the Braille models used at Perkins became celebrated in teaching circles for the blind and led to whimsical stories. One anecdote I heard on the campus was that a member of the Perkins faculty, while traveling in England, left his Braille maps in a taxi. They were picked up by a Scotland Yard detective who was certain he had found the blueprints of a spy intent upon sabotaging the British Empire!

Without question my favorite teacher in industrial arts was David Abraham, an Englishman who had made America his home. Today he serves as the chief engineer of the Howe Memorial Printing Press, enlisting his inventive genius in behalf of the sightless.

Mr. Abraham is a tall man with a clever face. My fingers somehow conveyed this cleverness to me. I studied auto mechanics under Mr. Abraham. At first I was clumsy in my efforts. I recall working with him one morning, timing a motor. In attempting to start the ignition, I placed my hand on the spark plugs and received a fifteen-hundred-volt shock from the engine. The jolt caused me to give an emphatic voluntary reflex and Mr. Abraham was deeply concerned. Although I was shaken, I pretended it had not bothered me at all.

Gradually I developed skill in my work. Mr. Abraham was able to give life to any subject he taught, no matter how dull it might seem to the beginner.

On one occasion I was assigned the task of dismantling the transmission of a Chevrolet engine, not an easy task even for a skilled mechanic. Mr. Abraham demonstrated how it was to be done, then showed me how to reassemble it. Finally he asked me whether I could do it without his help. When I assured him that I would try, he said, "Bob, I'll bet you twenty-five cents you cannot dismantle and reassemble this engine within an hour."

"I'll take the bet, Mr. Abraham. Twenty-five cents says I can!"

I reached feverishly for the parts in the steel case. Guided by memory and sensitivity of touch, I unscrewed the head of the motor, reached for the position of the valves and spark plugs in respect to the cylinders. I placed a tire iron under the valve rocket arm, forced the valves to open, and then traced the valve rods to their second seats on the camshaft eccentrics. Having disassembled the parts, I began the job of putting them together again. Visualizing the relationship of the flywheel to the pistons, the relationship of the cylinders to each other, the operation of the crankshaft through a complete firing cycle, I was able to reassemble each part into its normal position.

The entire operation had taken twenty minutes. I called Mr. Abraham over. He tested the completed mechanism and uttered an exclamation of surprise. "By God, Bob, how did you do it so quickly?"

"I simply memorized the job while you were showing me."

When Joe Jablonske called for me at the end of the class Mr. Abraham pressed the twenty-five cents into my hand and continued to mutter and shake his head.

In addition to my receiving private instruction in class, Joe Jablonske served as a private tutor in several subjects, helping me after class.

Joe possessed limited vision and had been at Perkins for twenty-five years, assuming the duties of an instructor after graduating as a student. There were times when I tried Joe's patience severely. Although I was bored by geometry, I had a secret incentive to study it thoroughly, simply to embarrass Joe. I could sense sometimes when I read my lessons, droning on and on by the hour, that his attention was wandering. I would feel his jaw sag, his head slip backward, and I had the impression that he was gazing absent-mindedly at the ceiling, his foot wagging idly. At such times I would slip in a few spurious laws of measure and design; and once when I turned a rhomboid into a "finigal"—a purely mythical figment of my imagination—my prank went entirely unnoticed.

There were times when I would pause in my reading and inquire with dubious innocence, "Am I right, Joe?"

"Read it to me again," he would reply, his fingers drumming on the desk, his head cocked to one side.

After my first year, when I began to attend classes with the other pupils, Joe accompanied me to my science studies to help me with the experiments. In physics, during our experiments with electricity, Mr. Cleveland, the teacher, hooked up batteries with a coil to show how the voltage could be stepped up. In a mischievous mood I took Joe's hand and pushed it suddenly on the bare wires. He leaped from the shock. But he did not cry out alone. I had forgotten to take my hand away from the apparatus and was caught in a second circuit. The jolt to me was an unexpected and a well-deserved one.

Joe was in his glory in history. He knew the subject so well that it was virtually impossible to deceive him on historical facts. However, I took grim satisfaction in ferreting out points on which we could differ, a tactic that resulted in explosive arguments. I loved to argue; it helped me to compare judgments and to add new words in verbal combat to those which I had recently learned. These mental clashes with Joe frequently reached a pitch of pandemonium.

"I know very well that the first usable railway was built in Pennsylvania," I insisted, "not in New York or New England."

"I tell you it wasn't built in Pennsylvania!"

"It was built there! I know it for a fact."

"Where did you read that?"

"I don't remember. But it was built there just as sure as you are Joe Jablonske."

This was finally verified by our going to the library. And when Miss Worth, the librarian, vindicated my assertion, I was beside myself with pleasure.

Joe would yield to me by grinning and giving me a sharp pinch in the ribs.

My teasing extended to every subject. When Joe asked me to read him Longfellow's poem, *The Song of Hiawatha*, I balked, saying that I had already read it once.

"Read it to me again, I want to hear it."

I had a brilliant inspiration. I read with one hand, pounded on the desk with the other in imitation of an Indian tom-tom, and deepened my voice into a guttural singsong.

>"By the shores of Gitche Gumee,
>   By the shining Big-Sea-Water . . . "

"Stop that!" Joe shouted, grabbing my hand from the line I was following. I simply ignored him, ran my other hand over the verse and went on reading in the same rhythmic monotone, adding the stamping of my feet to the thumping quality of my voice. He began to pinch me, as he usually did when exasperated, but I merely increased the speed of the rhythm. However, it couldn't last for long; Joe pushed the book away and closed it.

My social contacts at Perkins were naturally limited but rich and satisfying. My loneliness of other years was greatly lessened by activities and friendship. Leonard Dowdy and I were together much of the time, doing forbidden things. We would climb the pine trees in front of our cottage in violation of the rules and, in autumn at the height of the apple season, we would steal into the orchard behind the director's office with boxes and pick ripe apples. This orchard was one of the glories of Perkins. And it was fenced off precisely to prevent the plundering Leonard and I engaged in. However, we learned to hoist ourselves over the gate, helping each other to perform the trick. Soon we were lost among the thick branches of our favorite tree, one which had the sweetest fruit. When we felt the footsteps of Joe Jablonske thudding along the spongy turf in hot pursuit, we would move in close to the trunk under the lushly spreading branches; and when we were sure he was under the tree, we shook it violently, causing the apples to tumble over him.

Leonard and I sat opposite one another at meals and we devised a method for communication by tapping our feet in Morse code. The continual stamping caused annoyance to the matron who served the meals and to the other students, but it in no way dampened our enthusiasm. Suppertime was always the social high spot of our day. I can taste the deliciousness of the bread served at Perkins even now. I have

66

often believed it was prepared by the hands of angels. I still savor the memory of hot rolls with crisp, tasty crusts; the corn bread fresh from the oven with melted butter dripping from it; the banana bread and French bread and muffins.

Sunday mornings I attended chapel with Joe. Since it was impossible to speak aloud during the service, Joe used the manual alphabet and his flying fingers described everything that was taking place. The chapel was one of the loveliest buildings on campus. I have experienced much pleasure running my fingers over its graceful columns, fingering the splendid hardwood seats carved in straight grains and small curlicues with the natural finish. I have been told that the stained-glass window over the altar, depicting Jesus helping blind men, is beautiful to see as the sunlight filters through the colored pane. The services were non-sectarian. I stood beside Joe when the hymns were announced, and Joe always insisted that I sing with him. I am convinced that our duet together, mingling with the other voices, must have been grotesque to hear. Joe would sing in a high tenor and I, trying to compensate for this, would sing in a deliberately deep monotone. At the end of a hymn Joe would let loose a long, drawn-out "Amen" that would sink to a quivering groan. I tried my utmost to match it, but was seldom successful. Joe tried his best to make the service meaningful to me, but it was difficult and tiring to read the manual alphabet for two hours of speeches and prayers. The only relaxation I found was the soothing sound of the organ across the aisle. I would follow its rhythms and vibrations, trying to predict when the music would grow softer or louder, swifter or more leisurely. And, sometimes, when the vibrations became suddenly intense, the tears would come to my eyes as if sound had miraculously discarded its heavy impenetrable veil of silence, disclosing to my inner senses the chasteness of true melody, and my spirit had been lured to follow an invisible summons.

I felt this way always at the end of the service when the organ burst into "The Battle Hymn of the Republic," to the accompaniment of several hundred voices. "Glory, glory, hallelujah; His soul goes marching on." Even the deaf-blind can feel the galloping tones of that paean to eternity.

Music, for all its mystery and remoteness, held a strong allurement for me. In the tower of the chapel hung the Cartwright bells. There were eight of them, each weighing over two hundred pounds and tuned to the scale. The bells rang for Sunday service and on other festive occasions. One afternoon I made my way cautiously up the ladder into the belfry, followed by Leonard and Joe Jablonske. My hands explored these bells hanging silently in their iron frames. Curiously I investigated their wide, round mouths. I swung one of the clappers against the side of the bronze shell and was rewarded in the stillness of the bell chamber by a long vibrant stroke that sent a thrill through me. Moved beyond utterance, I picked my way down the ladder, re-entering into the thickening silence. On the morning after V-E Day, when Germany surrendered to the Allies, we pupils awoke to find one of the bells lying on the campus grounds. Apparently some celebrant, stimulated by liberal libations, had climbed to the belfry and brought the bronze giant to earth. But despite this impressive feat of a prankster, I realized in deep depression that only the shell, not the song, had been grounded. For me, the music remained perpetually beyond my reach.

However, during my years at Perkins, my exposure to continual companionship thawed my memories of loneliness, isolation, and the irrational fear of dark and secluded places that was an even more regressive expression of my insecurity.

When I entered Perkins there were two hundred and fifty pupils in residence from every part of the globe. Both Dr. Howe and Michael Agnanos had passed on. The third director, Dr. Edward Allen, who had moved the school from downtown Boston to its present site overlooking the Charles River in Watertown, had retired, and the school was under its fourth director, Dr. Gabriel Farrell.

Dr. Farrell had carried on the tradition of his predecessors, placing the students together in resident family groups, putting boys with partial vision in with the totally blind and the five deaf-blind students at school in with the hearing. Ordinarily the blind and the deaf-blind have very little in common with one another, and the blind have a tendency to look down upon the "children of the silent night," as we with double handicaps were called. However, after months of shyness, I began to mingle with several of the blind and made firm friends.

In some cases I was able to read their lips; in others they learned to speak the manual alphabet, and we spent many hours at night in bull sessions, discussing the various accidents and illnesses which had brought us to Perkins. One boy had been struck over the eye with a snowball and had developed a blood clot on the optic nerve; another had been playing with a stick of dynamite in his father's garage. The explosion had blown down one wall and ripped a gaping hole in the floor. He had been found in a river of blood, his face almost torn away, and it was months before the doctors could tell whether he would live. Another boy had lost his sight through spinal meningitis. Still another had been stabbed in the eyeball with scissors while playing with a school chum. Several had developed eye infections, living in the slums, and had gone blind when their parents, through ignorance, had failed to consult a doctor. Others could have had their sight conserved if they had been entered in time in sight-saving classes. A few were born blind and had no vision memories whatsoever. All of them, sooner or later, with the help of state scholarships, had found their way to Perkins.

I made friends with several who were genuine "characters." Eddie Murphy was one. In addition to his being blind, one leg was crippled and his left hand was paralyzed. But he rarely was despondent. Frequently, as we sat together on my bed, telling funny stories until midnight, Eddie would gossip about his relatives in Boston; he had hordes of relatives. When we parted for vacation, in virtually every letter he wrote he would announce that he had become an uncle again. Always some branch of the Murphys seemed to be increasing. He was a walking encyclopedia of obituary notices, keeping me posted on the death of every Hibernian of prominence in Boston. I loved Eddie's exuberance and his perverse Irish humor.

Freddie Hayashi, another friend, was a very different sort. A Japanese from Hawaii, short and plump with round fat cheeks, Freddie was completely blind and there was something about him that filled me with awe. Freddie insisted that the devil frequently came to his bedside at night, disguised as a gentleman in a shiny top hat. And when Freddie stared at him, he would laugh in a horrible mocking tone and change into a beautiful woman with expensive silks and jewels. Terrified, Freddie would dig his fists into his eyes to drive off the vision.

I made stimulating friendships with adults as well as students. Once while I was having a lesson with Miss Carpenter, my English teacher, I became aware that the door of the room had opened and someone had come in.

"Let me introduce you to Mr. Edmundson, Bob," Miss

Carpenter said. We stood up, and I shook hands with the stranger.

"Hello," he answered, placing my hand on his face. He was an individual of about medium height, slender and erect, with a rather thin face. Unlike other strangers I had met, he seemed completely at home with lip reading. There was a friendliness in his manner that put me at ease.

Miss Carpenter moved to another chair, and Mr. Edmundson sat down beside my desk.

"Where are you from?" I asked.

"I come from West Virginia, Bob."

"But you don't have a Southern drawl."

He laughed—a spontaneous, running laughter which intrigued me.

"Why are you at Perkins, Mr. Edmundson?"

"I have a little deaf-blind girl. Have you met 'Bimmy,' Bob?"

"No, I don't believe so."

"Her real name is Caroline, but we call her 'Bimmy.' She's only eight years old. She arrived here a few days ago."

In the course of our conversation I learned that Mr. Edmundson was a lawyer. He seemed high-strung; he smoked cigarettes in rapid succession, taking long puffs.

We talked for half an hour—about Pittsburgh, my home town, baseball, poetry. Mr. Edmundson had a splendid sense of humor. His mind quickly grasped the whimsical.

I met Bimmy the following morning. She was a quiet little girl; her entire attitude struck me as being passive and retreating. She had no speech whatsoever.

"Why do they call her 'Bimmy'?" I asked Miss Carpenter. "It's certainly an odd name."

Miss Carpenter explained that Mr. Edmundson had given

71

her the nickname from the word "cherubim" in the second verse of the hymn:

> Holy, holy, holy,
> All thy saints adore Thee,
> Casting down their golden crowns around the glassy sea.
> Cherubim and seraphim
> Falling down before Thee,
> Who wert and art and evermore shall be.

When Bimmy had been a baby her father had stroked her head and rocked her to sleep, singing this hymn to quiet her restlessness; and the name, springing from devoted affection, had ever since been hers.

Mr. Edmundson visited Perkins frequently, and we became friends. I looked forward to each new trip with enthusiasm. One afternoon he invited me to go with him to nearby Boston to watch the Red Sox. His exuberance was irresistible. He did not even give me time to change from my slacks into more presentable clothes. Within ten minutes he had brought his car around to the door of Tompkins Cottage, and we were on our way to Boston.

We took our seats in the grandstand at Fenway Park. I followed the game eagerly as he narrated the action, speaking into my thumb. His excited voice rose in resonance with each pitch. When an infielder made a skillful pickup, or the pitcher struck out a hitter, Mr. Edmundson would react as though he were seated on coiled springs, throwing his hands over his head in a yell. I came to understand what was meant by being a baseball fan. Before long I was as tense as he was, cheering Boston on vociferously. Between bites of frankfurters and hasty draughts of soda, I sat hunched in my seat, a bundle of nerves, scarcely daring to breathe when an opposing batter walked or made a hit, loudly speculating whether the batter who had just come up to the plate would knock the ball into the bleachers.

As time passed, I got to see increasingly more of "Bimmy." She would come into my study room with Juanita, a charming little deaf-blind girl, two years older than Bimmy, who was loved by everyone. Juanita spoke and had a pleasant personality, and she strove to make Bimmy sociable; but Bimmy seemed indifferent to everything. Juanita would push her forward so that I could greet her, but Bimmy would hang back, obviously not wishing to associate with me. There was an aloofness about her that made me curious.

"What on earth is the matter with Bimmy?" I asked Miss Carpenter.

"It's a tragedy." Miss Carpenter shook her head vigorously. "We are all at our wits' end with Bimmy. She's such a pretty little girl. But she doesn't seem to be able to learn anything. Mr. Edmundson would give years of his life to hear her say 'Father' just once."

"Well, she'll probably improve as time goes on."

But Bimmy didn't improve. Sometimes I would take her hand, place it on my lips and say, "Bimmy." Her invariable answer was a long drawn-out "Ooooooo." She would hang back, pulling away from me. The quality of strangeness in her never seemed to lift.

In the weeks that followed I brought Bimmy candy and sweets, tried to provoke in her a desire to communicate with me. But it was useless. Bimmy would fly into sudden rages, refuse to eat her meals; and once, in a fit of temper when I tried to take her hand and put some candy into it, she picked up a glass on my dresser and hurled it to the floor, smashing it into fragments.

The end was as tragic as it was inevitable. The doctors finally located Bimmy's trouble. Her problem was not her

73

physical handicaps, but her mind. She was taken from Perkins and placed in an asylum for the insane. I never heard of her again. But through the years I keep a memory of poor, kindly Mr. Edmundson and the song he had sung so hopefully over his sleeping baby.

> Holy, holy, holy,
> All thy saints adore Thee,
> Casting down their golden crowns
> Around the glassy sea. . . .

As a relief from my studies and other exercises in mental discipline, I had desired virtually from the time I entered Perkins to engage in some form of competitive sport. Two years before my coming Perkins had put together its first wrestling team, taking part in a round robin of contests with schools of the seeing as well as the blind. Wrestling offered a definite challenge to me. I knew I was in perfect physical condition, possessing strength that was above the average for boys my own age.

But when I relayed my ambition to Ralph Feliciano, my attendant, he shook his head. "Are you crazy? No deaf-blind person has ever succeeded in becoming a wrestler. They won't let you try out for the team."

When I approached Mrs. Nilsson, the head of the deaf-blind department, she, too, opposed it. But when I persisted in pursuing the subject she reluctantly gave me permission to report for practice.

Jubilantly I made arrangements to attend the team's next workout. When my ambitions became known to the wrestlers, one of them, Walter, came to my room to administer a lesson. Walter grabbed me suddenly by the shoulders, and in an instant I found myself stretched across my bed, his strong, short arms pinioning my arms against my sides. My pre-

liminary surprise (and shock) passed into rage. I was mortified at being held so unceremoniously on my back. I struggled to free myself, but my erratic, undisciplined exertions
only tightened the hold Walter had taken. He held me immobile for nearly five minutes—long enough for me to realize
that wrestling was much more than a display of berserk
strength. Walter weighed only one hundred and twenty
pounds; he was thirty pounds lighter than I. But he was
strong and nimble.

When he had loosened his grip and permitted me to get on
my feet, he smiled. "Bobby, I thought I'd teach you the
fundamentals of wrestling by actual performance."

Instead of dampening my spirits, this first hint of real
wrestling merely whetted my appetite for more. Wrestling
practice was held the following evening. Walter offered to
take me over to the gymnasium at eight o'clock. As the time
approached, I grew so excited that my heart beat like a trip
hammer. I kept opening my watch to feel the time, not
convinced that it was accurate, fretfully counting the minutes.

I had borrowed a pair of wrestling tights from one of the
boys on the team, but they felt oddly constricting and not a
little incongruous. They made me think of the tight casings
used for frankfurters.

Down in the gym I found Mr. Di Martino, the coach,
waiting for me. He took me to the center of the big mat,
stretched himself out comfortably on his stomach, and told
me to turn him over. For fully ten minutes I tugged and
pulled at him without success. Mr. Di Martino seemed to be
as flexible as an eel and just as unmanageable. Whenever I
seemed on the point of flipping him onto his back he would
simply shift his weight and return to his former position. He

was obviously enjoying himself; I could feel him quivering with laughter at every futile assault I made.

"All right," I finally sputtered, thoroughly exhausted. "It's absolutely useless. We're only wasting time. Just *how* do you turn a wrestler onto his back and keep him there?"

In an instant I found myself being levered onto my shoulders. I struggled frantically to hold my position; I clawed at the mat cover, but my fingers found no holds. In one quick twist I was pinned helplessly on my back, my arms and legs flailing the air like pistons. I subsided, more aware now than ever there was more to this art of wrestling than brute force.

I spent the rest of the evening—and many other evenings —absorbing the assaults of the other boys. It was a prolonged study in trial and error, yet I was determined to learn. Although my elbows and knees became painfully abraded from my continual mauling on the heavy cotton cover of the mat, I refused to concede that my case was hopeless. Gradually I learned how to defend myself against nelsons, the cradle, and the figure-four scissors.

During my first full year at Perkins I practiced running on the circular track, punching the bag, exercising with pulleys, and lifting weights. I did finger-tip pushups and situps. Slowly my reflexes became more rapid; I developed an instinctive muscular balance, an intuitive sense which told me when an opponent was shifting to a new hold. I learned to block on the defensive; studied all the methods used by others in making their opening attacks. My sense of touch became keener, my balance and posture improved as I learned to control my muscles at will.

However, whatever hopes I had of making the team in my sophomore year were dissipated during the elimination contests which took place before the season opened. In my first bout I was wrestled out of the one-hundred-and-fifty-five-pound class by Wayne, a boy who had considerable experience. I was desperately disappointed. I even thought of abandoning my hopes of making the team.

Mr. Di Martino saw me sitting despondently on the bench with my hands on my head. He came over and put his arm around me. "Keep on practicing, Bobby. Don't give up."

I looked up, my eyes filled with tears. "What's the use, Mr. Di Martino? I guess I was mistaken from the first about my chances."

"You'll make the team yet, Bobby. Don't ever tell yourself anything else."

And so I returned to the gym and went through another season with the pulleys, lifting weights, practicing holds. Night after night I climbed a twenty-foot rope to develop my arms, hands, and shoulders. Sitting erect, placing hands behind my head, I dropped back until my head touched the mat, and sat up again, leaning as far forward as possible. I did these situps fifty times a night.

My confidence and good spirits returned. When the day for the elimination bouts approached, the following fall, I knew that I had improved tremendously. Walter, possibly the best wrestler on the team, seemed much less formidable to me in practice. In several trials, neither of us was able to pin the other to the mat, perhaps because we were both acquainted with the same techniques. When the time came for choosing the team my confidence was so unshakable that I did not even take the preliminary warmup. My bout was with Wayne, the boy who had beaten me previously. As we locked arms, Wayne, who had partial vision, tried to use his old technique—a quick, lifting, twisting motion which previously had slammed me to the mat with a thud. But I didn't wait for it. I dropped to one knee, dove through his guard and gripped his ankles. I jerked hard; Wayne lost his balance and fell backward in a flying sprawl. In an instant I was with him, catching his head and arm in a nelson that pulled him over so that his buttocks rose into the air and his head was firmly planted between his knees. It seemed so simple that I could not resist chuckling over it. Within seconds my hand was being pumped by the members of the squad and the coach put his arm around my shoulders with an affectionate squeeze. I had made the team.

Before our first match of the season, with Needham High School, I spent hours running in the gym, swinging on the ladders and stall bars. Fearing I might gain weight and step out of my class, I went into a rigorous diet which excluded breadstuffs, sweets, and potatoes.

When we arrived in the gym at Needham for the match I was nervous with pent-up excitement. I tried to dress leisurely, but I felt as though I were running a fever. Willie Shelnutt, our new coach—Mr. Di Martino had recently left us—kept patting my shoulder. "Take it easy now. Save your strength. We'll win this match."

Finally we took our seats in a row alongside the mat, facing the other team across the width of canvas. The bouts began with the lighter weights. I was scheduled to wrestle three contests before the end. Though I couldn't see the activity in front of me, my imagination would not let me rest. I kept picturing the straining, writhing torsos as they pushed and turned and shifted. I could feel the dull thud of feet as they braced against the mat; the fall of bodies when they collided and went down.

A few minutes before my turn Willie came over to give some final advice. "Remember, Bob, the referee will tap you once on the shoulder to begin; two taps means you are to stop wrestling. Is that clear?"

I met my seeing opponent—a boy named Cuppinger—in

the middle of the mat. We shook hands, and I noticed that his hand was as cold as mine. Then we took the referee's position and waited. The single tap came abruptly; we locked together.

I immediately discovered that Cuppinger was a few inches taller than I was, with powerfully developed muscles. I was forced to use all the wiles I knew, feinting with my feet and hands to throw him off guard. Disengaging from him, I moved in, keeping my body in a low crouching position, reaching for my opponent's waist. My arms caught him at the midriff; I shifted my hip and swung. We fell to the mat with a thud, but I was on top. I immediately began my favorite hold—the figure-four scissors. I swung my right leg over and around his body, hooking my foot behind my left knee. I tried for a pinning nelson, but he managed to squirm his way onto the floor. However, keeping my legs wrapped relentlessly around his waist, I applied strong pressure. I pulled him over on his side so that his shoulders touched the mat. Two quick taps on my shoulder told me that the match was over. I stood bruised and shaken, the sweat pouring from my body. The referee raised my hand over my head. I had won.

This triumph over Cuppinger gave me decided prestige on the Perkins campus. The student body seemed to regard me with esteem. The younger boys, in particular, displayed an attitude of hero worship. Naturally I was flattered, but I was not inclined to rest upon my laurels.

As the team made preparations for its next match, I awoke one morning to find that the index finger on my left hand was badly swollen and painful. I showed it to Willie Shelnutt.

"Bob, you'd better go over to the clinic for an examination."

The doctor examined the finger and found that it was not broken, nor was there any sign of infection. He was puzzled. He put it into a splint. After a few days without any visible improvement I was sent to a specialist at one of the Boston hospitals.

He suspected arthritis. "You'll have to take a complete rest," he advised.

When Mrs. Nilsson heard the verdict she declared, "Well, Bobby, you'll have to give up wrestling."

For a day I sulked in my room. Then, heedless of the advice and the well-meant reproaches, I sneaked in my practice in the gym at odd hours, exercising with the pulleys and weights. Apparently I adopted the right cure. Under my exercise, the pain left the finger and only the swelling remained. I wrestled with this swollen finger in several matches. Eventually it returned to normal.

One of the most exciting matches of the year was with Phillips Academy at Andover. The academy had always had a fine team, and we were especially eager to beat them. Our team traveled to Andover by truck; it was a rough, cold ride in the heart of the winter. It was a seven-bout contest. At the end of the fifth bout the teams were tied. Players and spectators alike were tense under the strain of the seesaw competition. I was scheduled to wrestle next. I had already taken my warm-up exercise, and I was sitting on the bench wrapped in a blanket to keep up the sweat, when the coach came over to me. "Bob, I'm going to put Norman in your place now. I want to save you for the final match."

"But Norman is chiefly a defensive player. He's weak on attack."

"We'll let Norman ride this out and hope for a draw. Then it will be up to you, Bob, to pin the final man."

My stomach grew queasy at the thought of this sudden responsibility.

Norman drew his match just as Willie had predicted and the score remained tied. As I walked onto the mat, striving to control my jitters, I knew that I had to win this one.

My opponent was a speedy, powerful fellow who shifted his techniques with ease to meet the changing situation. As soon as I received the signal to begin I moved in, keeping my body low. As my opponent moved for my legs, I jumped back, coming to the mat on both knees. Simultaneously I hooked my arms underneath both of his shoulders. He wiggled loose and put me under him, trying for a pinning hold. But I broke it by rolling over on my hip until he was underneath me. I fought to maintain my weight on him and keep him off balance. He threw his legs up over his head, thrashing in an attempt to wriggle free. I was growing desperately tired; my throat felt as though it would burst. But my opponent was weakening even more than I. With his last bit of strength he tried to shake loose by pulling his shoulder and arm between our bodies. But I squeezed tight with a cradle hold, rolled him over, and just as he came in contact with the mat, I reached him through my leg and scissored him above the knee. My head swam dizzily, but I smiled for I knew I had won. Within seconds the referee raised my arm to make it official. Before the stunned Andover crowd, Perkins had pulled out the match 23 to 20.

During my last year of competition complications arose. While walking to classes I slipped on a patch of ice and badly sprained my ankle. We had a match scheduled with the Overlea School for the Blind only two weeks away. But with my ankle swollen to twice its size, it seemed improbable that I would be able to recuperate in time. The physician treated it with cold packs and special diathermy and taped it with a bandage. I had my shoes on by the end of the first week and insisted on practicing prior to leaving for the South.

One afternoon as I sat dejectedly with my foot in the whirlpool bath, two of the boys came over and told me they were quitting the team.

I could hardly believe I had heard them correctly. "Have you gone off your rockers?"

"We're fed up with things. We've had enough of Shelnutt's rule that we can't smoke during the season."

"Willie didn't make the rule. It was passed down to him by the principal. He's merely carrying out orders."

"Well, that's too bad. And we're not the only guys who've had our bellyful. There are at least five other fellows ready to quit along with us."

Shelnutt was aware of the rebellion that was developing and he was worried. Before the next practice session, he came over to me.

"What am I going to do, Bobby? You can't force a man to wrestle when his heart isn't in it."

"Call a special meeting, Mr. Shelnutt, and let me speak to the boys."

When the meeting was called the rebel ringleaders refused to admit publicly to Shelnutt that smoking was the issue. They fell back on the excuse that they were no longer interested in the sport; that there was no time to practice, with their heavy schedules of study. I had always been hesitant about addressing a group of people. Indeed, with my speech handicap, public speaking absolutely unnerved me. However, I had asked Willie to let me address the team and I determined to go through with it. "Look, fellows, stop squaring off. You're quitting only because of the rule against smoking. You think your personal liberties are at stake. But what about Willie Shelnutt? Who do you suppose is going to suffer most by your action? He's been a grand coach, a wonderful friend to every one of us. Aren't you ashamed to play this kind of trick on him?"

I paused. "Look, fellows, we have a match against Overlea next week. My ankle is on the bum. Somebody is going to have to take my place when we go against those fellows. Who will it be?"

One of the fellows, George, spoke up. "I think we ought to take a vote, Bob, to see just how the fellows feel about it."

"That's right. I'm waiting to see who's going to be the first to hand in his uniform."

I guess there was no answer to that one. The vote was taken and the boys agreed unanimously to remain on the team.

With the rebellion quashed, Willie Shelnutt took his wrestlers to Overlea, brimming with confidence. My ankle improved to the point where I was able to take part in the match; however, something new hampered me. During the final practice session I got a severe mat burn across my chin, which formed a large incrustation.

"You'd better be careful," our trainer warned. "That burn will break open as soon as you rub your chin on the mat. Try to keep your head up—don't let the other fellow force it down."

As luck would have it, however, I had been wrestling for only a minute on the night of the match when my chin struck the top of my opponent's head. I felt a warm trickle of blood coursing down my chin and along my chest. The referee stopped us.

"Do you want to quit?" the coach asked, as soon as he came over.

"Why should I quit? I've only been in action for a minute."

"Your face is bleeding like a river. The mat is covered with blood. Better stop before it gets worse."

83

"Can't you find any bandages?"

"If you want to keep on, they will have the doctor tape it."

I decided to continue. The doctor in charge of the evening came over and put a liberal amount of iodine into the burn; it stung like a heated iron.

We resumed wrestling again, but the bandage across my chin proved to be a continual nuisance. Perspiring with effort, I kept fingering the flimsy thing; it would rub loose, first on one side and then on the other, so that I had to pause to press it back into place. Finally I decided to leave it alone. I lost the contest by a point. But, under the circumstances, I wasn't despondent. I had long since come to accept the downs as well as the ups of wrestling.

Looking back on my wrestling at Perkins, I must say that the thrills far outweighed the heartaches. And that is how it was with almost everything else I did there.

During my senior year I became close friends with Miss Alice Carpenter, the English teacher, to whom I have already referred. I have never met any person, young or old, who displayed Miss Carpenter's enthusiasm for life, her eagerness to learn and develop new interests, and her willingness to share her experiences with others.

For many years prior to World War II, Miss Carpenter had been head of the Ming Sum Missionary School for the Blind, located in Canton in South China. During the bombing of Canton she had placed her blind children on a houseboat under protection of a United States gunboat on Pearl River and, returning to the Ming Sum compound alone, opened it as a center for eight hundred Chinese refugees, despite the threats of the Japanese military commander and the ominously raised bayonets of the Nipponese soldiers.

On a number of occasions when Japanese patrols attempted to climb over the fence of the compound to molest the Chinese women within, this dynamic, gray-haired woman defied their bayonets, reminded them she was an American citizen, and warned them that they could only enter by using force. When hostilities finally broke out between Japan and the United States, Miss Carpenter refused to be evacuated along with the other citizens. She insisted on staying with her blind children, the only white person left in Canton. She was seized by the Japs, suffered agonizing weeks of internment, and finally was placed forcibly aboard the Swedish liner *Stockholm* bound for the United States. Upon landing, unable to continue her work for the Chinese blind in China, Miss Carpenter joined the department of the deaf-blind at the Perkins institute, and I had the privilege of becoming her first pupil.

Most people, after reaching a certain age, seem to lose their ability to adapt to new interests and new surroundings; but Miss Carpenter, despite her harrowing experiences in China, adjusted to the life at Perkins cheerfully. And she retained her capacity for enjoying life. During the winter of 1945–46, and after I had graduated from Perkins and gone to New York, we often went out together, visiting the landmarks so dear to the hearts of Americans. We explored the Old North Church in Boston where Paul Revere sounded his alarm to the minutemen; we climbed the Statue of Liberty, visited the tomb of Alexander Hamilton, inspected the sculptured animals at the Museum of Natural History in New York. We dined at Italian, Swedish, Chinese, and Japanese restaurants. Miss Carpenter introduced me to pea-pod soup, sukiyaki, and bean curd; we sampled the enticements of Smörgåsbord and the Italian delicacies.

Whenever Miss Carpenter saw an object that might interest me she found ways to show it to me or to describe it in detail. On our trips to Chinatown in Boston we stopped at the curio shops to finger the ivory, porcelains, silks, and carvings in sandalwood and teak.

I had fun in Miss Carpenter's English classes. I loved to read poetry. As early as the third grade I had written my first, childish verses. Poetry gave me the opportunity to explore with mental eyes many variations of the physical world. However, I had no patience with being asked to memorize poems simply because they were considered by others to be classics. It was more agreeable to enjoy poems because they were meant to be enjoyed.

"Bob, I want you to memorize this stanza from Wordsworth's *Immortality*," Miss Carpenter told me one afternoon. "Listen while I read it.

> "Our birth is but a sleep and a forgetting:
> The Soul that rises with us, our life's Star,
> Hath had elsewhere its setting,
> And cometh from afar:"

"Great God, I'd rather be a pagan!" I quoted from the same Wordsworth. "I've read that poem many times—and enjoyed reading it, too. But memorizing it—that takes all the life out of it. Why should I commit it to memory?"

"Oh, Bob, it's a beautiful stanza."

In the end I grudgingly memorized the stanza. Another thing I objected to was the practice of tracing poetry back to its so-called "sources" in the fashion of literary critics who continually prattle about how this poet was influenced by that poet.

I loved poetry for its own sake, stripped of scholarly annotations. When we studied Keats, for instance, I became very attached to one stanza:

86

I cannot see what flowers are at my feet,
Nor what soft incense hangs upon the boughs,
But in embalmed darkness I guess each sweet
Wherewith the seasonable month endows
The grass, the thicket, and the fruit-tree wild;
White hawthorne and pastoral eglantine;
Fast-fading violets, cover'd up in leaves;
And mid-May's eldest child,
The coming musk-rose, full of dewy wine,
The murmurous haunt of flies on summer eves.

This stanza seemed to exemplify my own emotional responses whenever I was confronted by nature and its loveliness in springtime. I would have given a year of life to have written it. This was also the case with the opening lines of Keat's other masterpiece, *Ode to a Grecian Urn:* I admired it for its wonder of pictorial beauty contrived from nothing more than a carven marble vase in Kensington Gardens. Keats and Shelley seemed to capture the music of my soul more precisely than any of the other poets I had read. In my idle moments I too dreamed the dreams that belong to "faerie lands unknown."

In our discursive reading, Miss Carpenter introduced me to a number of playwrights. We read Ibsen's *Doll's House*, Sir James Barrie's *Quality Street*, the plays of Sheridan and Shakespeare. Shakespeare, with his massive humanity, became my favorite. We read *Othello* twice, I think; and many times I found myself quoting that pointed, cryptic passage from Macbeth:

By the pricking of my thumbs,
Something wicked this way comes.

The archaic words one finds sprinkled through Shakespeare invariably aroused my curiosity; I looked into the glossaries and compared them with our modern equivalents. The lofty passages, so oddly eloquent, helped me to gain a clearer insight into the minds of mature humans. No wonder the psychologists—and even psychiatrists like Dr. Karl Menninger—frequently quote Elizabethan writings with such admiration.

The first week of classes Miss Carpenter made a valiant effort to interest me in A. E. Housman. Someone had presented her with a copy of *A Shropshire Lad*. The poems depressed me, despite their quaint, original rhythms. She insisted on having me memorize several short ones, but I was stanchly rebellious.

"Why bother with memorizing a lot of Welsh names like Omne and Teme and Clun? Nobody ever heard of them until Housman decided to mention them."

It delighted me to sit quietly pretending that I was reading her lips, while she was prattling on about Housman, when I was actually thinking of other things. Every now and then, I'd nod my head and say, "Good; fine." But my mind was elsewhere. In this respect, lip reading is much more convenient than hearing by ear. By ear you must listen to many things you don't want to hear. In lip reading one can shut his mind and feel nothing but a meaningless buzzing at the end of his fingers.

We had heated combats over the meaning of words. Sometimes we dickered over a single verb for hours before we agreed to consult a dictionary as a final norm for its sense. While I was writing a senior essay dealing with the three romantic poets, Shelley, Keats, and Wordsworth, we had opposite opinions as to whether I should use the word "imbued" or the word "endowed," in discussing a quality of Keats's poetry. I maintained that, since we were dealing with the impersonal quality of his work, the correct word should be "imbued." Miss Carpenter thought otherwise. We resorted to the dictionary but discovered that the difference between the two words was merely a matter of shading. We then consulted Miss Haven, another teacher of English, and I was gratified to discover that she seconded my choice. "I told you so," I exclaimed triumphantly.

The most controversial poet Miss Carpenter and I tackled was Robert Browning. I had been drawn to Browning's shorter lyrics—particularly those written in clear unambiguous language; while Miss Carpenter was inclined to defend his longer and more mystic poems. "Browning is one of the best of England's Victorian poets, Bob."

"And one of the least communicative, Miss Carpenter. How can one appreciate such obscure, gnarled language if one does not understand it?"

"It isn't obscure—it's exalted."

We would continue these arguments to the extreme, neither of us giving in. To prove her point, Miss Carpenter would ask me to read *Rabbi Ben Ezra*, or *My Last Duchess*.

"But, Miss Carpenter! These are not the poems I meant— I meant the others. *Sordello*, for instance. Who understands *Sordello*? Browning admitted he did not understand it after he had written it."

One afternoon she invited me to visit Craigie House in Cambridge, the historic mansion which had been Washington's headquarters during the Revolution and which had later become the home of Henry Wadsworth Longfellow, the poet.

We made this first pilgrimage to Craigie House in January of my senior year at Perkins. My initial impression of the house was one of spaciousness and age. The rooms are large; the furnishings had been practically unchanged for more than a century; the halls were filled with that odd odor which is a mixture of life and decay. The floors dipped where the years had warped them; and every so often one's footsteps creaked on the loose boards. I ran my fingers over old, unfamiliar carvings of wood, measured the furniture with curious hands, and was extremely delighted by the charming atmosphere.

While Miss Carpenter and I were wandering about Longfellow's study, inspecting even the smallest objects, an individual appeared in the doorway. I noticed that Miss Carpenter was talking to him; I stopped looking at the old desk I had been examining and waited.

"Bob, this is Professor Dana." Miss Carpenter directed my hand to greet him. "He is one of Longfellow's grandsons. Do you remember Edith in Longfellow's poem, *The Children's Hour?*"

"Certainly—Edith with the golden hair."

"Well, the professor is one of her children."

"Oh—but the name Dana. Does it have anything to do with the author who wrote the sea story—you know the one I mean."

"You're right!" Miss Carpenter rejoined. "The Danas and the Longfellows were connected by marriage."

Professor Dana seemed deeply interested in our tour; he took us through parts of the mansion not ordinarily open to the public. We saw the old clock on the stairs; the little chairs which had belonged to the Longfellow children; busts of the poet and his wife; and the bric-a-brac Longfellow had collected during his lifetime. Professor Dana permitted me to touch many objects which are carefully guarded in glass cases —books of the first editions of the poet's works, small art treasures and beautiful things which I had not dreamed existed. I was especially fascinated by a lovely agate cup, polished as thin as the finest chinaware, supported on a carved golden base, with gryphons curling over its edge in the shape of twisted handles. It had been made during the Renaissance by the "golden rogue," Benvenuto Cellini. It was so extraordinarily fragile and fine in its craftsmanship that I held it for several moments without knowing exactly what to say to express my admiration.

In Longfellow's study we found many nostalgic remembrances which the poet had treasured: an old writing desk that had belonged to Coleridge; the chair made from the wood of the "spreading chestnut tree"; the poet's old pipe, lying alongside a wooden box of tobacco, the tobacco nearly reduced to the dust that had mingled with it. There were souvenirs of his journeys, knicknacks from Europe. I felt strange moving in a room which had lost the warmth and friendliness of life, trying to picture the personality of a man through the testimony of the relics he had left to posterity.

Professor Dana showed me a bronze statue standing near a table in Longfellow's study. "Who do you think this would be?" He used the oral method of communication for the first time. He had an unusually pleasant speaking voice—deep, resonant, yet with a certain softness which I found attractive.

I fingered the statue carefully. "I don't know."

"I think you do," Professor Dana urged. "Try again."

"What are these small things on his feet?" I inquired. "They look like wings."

"They are wings. And who is *he*?"

"I'm afraid I can't guess."

"Do you know any Greek mythology?"

"Oh yes! I've read quite a bit of it."

"Don't you know which of the gods was winged like this?"

"Wings on his feet? Why, Hermes, the winged messenger of the gods!"

The professor smiled. "Exactly. Now let's enter the Hall of Statues."

In the Hall of Statues I was fascinated by the marble busts Professor Dana showed us. There were the heads of Washington, Longfellow, and several other splendid pieces. One of these was especially interesting to me: it was a sculptured head standing out from the center of a flower. "Is it Clytie?"

"Yes, it is," answered the professor. "But how did you know?"

"I couldn't think of any other figure like this in mythology."

This head of Clytie excited me; I recalled, suddenly, the beautiful legend of the lovely girl who fell in love with Apollo, and whom the sun god changed into a sunflower. And along with the legend came to mind the verses of Thomas Moore's Irish melody.

No, the heart that has truly lov'd never forgets,
But as truly loves on to the close,
As the sun-flower turns, on her god, when he sets,
The same look which she turn'd when he rose.

"Bob," said Professor Dana, "if you could guess who Clytie was, I wonder if you could discover who this other statue might be."

We moved across the hall and the professor placed my hand on another sculptured face. I knew it was a woman by the narrow rounded features of the head—the full, small lips, the delicate nose. My fingers slipped downward, following the graceful neck and shoulders. Suddenly I stopped, a hot flush of embarrassment suffusing my face.

"Well, Bob," said Miss Carpenter, "why are you blushing?"

"It's—it's not dressed!" I stammered. "It's nude."

"Who is it?"

"Venus, of course."

"How do you know?"

"How could I help but know? Who else would have a face like that—and be portrayed without clothes?"

Several weeks after our first visit to Craigie House, Miss Carpenter and I saw Professor Dana again, in the old study where we first met him, wandering among his treasured possessions. Professor Dana was a member of the Harvard faculty, a professor of Russian literature. Miss Carpenter, it seemed, had told him that I was devoted to the poetry of John Keats, and now he proposed that we visit the Keats Room in the Houghton Library of Rare Manuscripts at Harvard University. It was a dismal day to go anywhere, with snow falling slowly but steadily; still, the temptation of seeing the Keats Room—and especially the beautiful death mask of Keats himself—easily overcame our apprehensions about the weather. We set out for Harvard, our collars up, our hands gloved, and our courage high in spite of the impending storm.

We were glad to arrive at the Harvard library, with its inviting warmth and the musty odor of old leather bindings hanging in the air like an antique breath. The Keats Room proved to be a beautiful chamber situated in the heart of the library; it was finished in black-walnut paneling, with built-in bookcases on three sides of the room. Opposite the heavy double doors was a marble fireplace, above which, in a niche of the molded mantel of fine wood, Keats looked down in marble, with closed eyes. I was touched when Miss Steele, Curator of the Keats Collection, permitted me to hold several fragile old manuscripts, all written by Keats. The papers were worn and dry with age, carefully and beautifully preserved in rich bound-leather cases. Here was his immortal sonnet which began:

> When I have fears that I may cease to be
> Before my pen has glean'd my teeming brain.

And here, too, were pages from *Endymion* and several other poems in their original manuscripts. I held them in my hands proudly, careful not to let my fingers break the crumbling sheets.

Professor Dana had to leave to attend to business, but Miss Carpenter and I stayed on with Miss Steele, wandering from case to case, satisfying our curiosity with snatches of letters written by Keats and by friends of the poet. Unfortunately it was difficult for me to follow the longer letters; lip reading is far from conducive to an extended session of reading because of the position of the hand and arm.

"Well, Bob, what did you think of it?" Miss Carpenter asked me as we left the library and went out into the stormy evening.

"There is nothing like fingering the manuscripts of a poet you admire; it is like looking over his shoulder while he writes them."

The snow was coming down more heavily now; the pavements were thickly covered with a white, cold mantle of softness. We took the subway train for Boston and threaded our way through the late-afternoon throng to Pierone's restaurant, celebrated for its sea food. When we arrived, after a ten-minute walk through the drifting snow, we found ourselves covered from head to foot with crystals. We were glad for the comfortable cheeriness of the room, the pervading odors of hot food, and nothing could have been more delightful than to remove our wet, chilly coats, which felt like damp shrouds. We both ordered swordfish. The pangs of hunger were so keen that we devoured the rolls that were brought in a small basket before the main dish had arrived.

As the meal progressed and our sense of well-being grew, I asked for a pencil and composed verses on Keats, inspired by my visit of the afternoon. It was a sonnet, not an exceptionally good one, I thought, but one which satisfied my desire to express my mood. Strangely enough, this sonnet is now in the Keats Collection itself. I would never have dreamed it possible, but Miss Steele included it among those papers.

It was nearly nine o'clock when Miss Carpenter and I set out for Perkins. We took a trolley to Watertown; the snow was coming down in a soft, enveloping mass now. The fluffy white flakes filtered into everything; our coats became a frosted mass of them, and no matter how often we shook ourselves, new snowflakes would soon cling tenaciously to our shoulders. It was bitterly cold. Furthermore, several crowded trolleys went by before one stopped for us.

The trolley seemed to crawl along, halting frequently until the way was cleared by snowplows. What should have been a journey of only thirty minutes lengthened into an hour, then two hours. Finally the car came to a halt altogether; even the plows had ceased working because of the deepening drifts. We sat, huddled together for warmth, wondering what course to take now that there seemed no chance of our reaching Perkins before midnight.

"Bob, what *are* we going to do?"

"Walk, of course."

"We can't walk. It's still a long way from the school."

"But Miss Carpenter, it's terribly cold here. It can't be any colder outside."

We climbed out of the trolley and began to plunge doggedly through the knee-deep drifts.

"Oh, Bob, I can't see!"

"What do you mean? Are you snow-blind?"

"No, but the snow is coming down so thickly that I can't see more than a few feet ahead."

"A little way is better than nothing, you know. But if you see a place where we can eat, Miss Carpenter, let's stop in. I'm so starved I could eat anything that sizzles."

Neither of us kept track of time while we plodded along, trying to keep under the shelter of trees or in the ruts made by passing vehicles. We would raise our feet high into the air, take a long step—and usually plunge into a deeper bank of snow. Both of us fell from time to time; it was impossible to maintain equilibrium in that shifting white mass. Snow penetrated into our clothing, sifting down through our collars and into our shoes. Miraculously we found a small diner along the road.

We ordered hot sandwiches and strong coffee. Between bites of food, I muttered, "I don't see why poets have always been so lyrical about the snow. While raving about its beauties, they were probably popping corn and roasting chestnuts by crackling firesides. I think I'd rather have an oil burner than a poem; it's much more efficient on nights like this."

When we went out into the night again the wind had lessened; the snow was still falling, but it seemed less forceful than before. Feeling refreshed after our meal, we attacked the deep drifts with renewed vigor.

It was very late when we entered the Northbeacon Gate at the edge of the Perkins campus. The snow was deeper here, for the wind had drifted it under the sheltering boughs of the big elms and the pines; and now that the wind was asleep, the whiteness stretched away across the grounds in an unbroken silent surface. Like being in a church, I thought.

We said good night at the door of Tompkins Cottage; I climbed the circular stairs from the lobby to my room, slipping out of my coat as I walked through the hall. I felt my watch: nearly two o'clock. I slipped into bed and huddled snugly down in my blankets.

I did not meet Professor Dana again until spring was well advanced; true, we wrote to each other, but he was invariably busy delivering lectures on his illustrious grandsire or on the Russian drama. Then, toward the end of April, he telephoned Miss Carpenter and invited us to visit Longfellow's grave in Mt. Auburn Cemetery.

It was a cold, bleak Sunday that we chose to visit the famous old burying grounds in Cambridge. The city of the dead was still desolate with a late spring; wind caught at stray strands of wisteria vines and tossed the branches of trees whose leaves were just beginning to bud. The chill of the afternoon and the tempestuous, blustering wind wrought a spell of loneliness over the great necropolis, so that even I, who could neither see nor hear, felt the loneliness of the scene. Examining the old tomb—a sepulcher with carved edges—I thought how poignantly isolated a human life becomes when it is separated from the world of animate things. "The dead are so terribly dead when they have died," I remarked to Miss Carpenter.

Later, after we had returned to Craigie House, I wandered about the old mansion trying to crystallize the experience I had undergone at the grave. I stepped with Miss Carpenter out of the house into a beautiful old-fashioned garden. The sun was already setting, but the evening, soft as a child's breath, was permeated with the odor of damp warm earth and young green life. I have never seen a garden as peaceful as the one where Longfellow used to walk.

The picket fences were covered with climbing roses, and masses of them hung over the gate in scented tangles of bloom. The carefully groomed beds were full of iris and columbine, interspersed with dainty forget-me-nots and old sweet lavender. The paths were narrow and winding, bordered by trim little box hedges, and here and there were flowering shrubs like dwarf sentries on guard. In the background, soaring upward with their years of hardy age, the pines kept watch as they had been keeping watch for many seasons. I placed my hand on the trunk of an old tree; the wind was silent but the supple branches still whispered, sending a tremor through the living wood.

"Is it dark, Miss Carpenter?"

"No, Bob—there is still light. But the light is very soft and gray."

"Twilight, then. So the soft gray face of evening is our guide."

The atmosphere was permeated with a heavy cloud of perfume hanging like a giant censer in the night. It was one of the rarest evenings I had ever spent.

I saw the professor once again before I graduated. He came to dinner at Perkins, for we had invited him to be our guest in recognition of the pleasure he had brought to us. And I still remember, after all these years, his last remarks.

"Robert," he began, using the formal approach that always indicated the gravity of his mood, "you must never give up your hope of going to college and becoming a writer. Remember that you must always keep an open mind. There will be those who do not understand you, but try to understand *them*."

As for Miss Carpenter, I have continued to cherish the friendship of this wise, sympathetic woman through the years.

There is one last experience with Miss Carpenter I would like to mention before I go on to other matters.

The summer following my graduation from Perkins, Miss Carpenter invited me to spend a vacation with her at Dream Canyon in the heart of the Rocky Mountains.

Midway in August we started on our trip. On the way to Dream Canyon we stopped for a few days in Hastings, Nebraska, to visit Miss Carpenter's father and two aunts. I enjoyed meeting Aunt Nina, a fragile person, but a bundle of energy; and also Aunt Janet, a professor of English at a nearby college. But I spent my most stimulating hours with Miss Carpenter's father, whom we all called "Dad." I walked with him along the parkway under the trees or stood gossiping with him on the front lawn. Mr. Carpenter told me many stories about the days when he had been a sheepherder on the range.

From Hastings we traveled on to Dream Canyon, where Marie Stoddard, Miss Carpenter's cousin, joined us to complete the party. Marie was a tall, friendly woman with a sweet voice that sounded like a little girl's.

This was my first experience in the high mountains, and I was excited by the change of altitude. The day before reaching Dream Canyon we had been complaining about the heat of the lowlands; now the weather was delightfully cool.

We camped in a rocky glen nine thousand feet above sea level, studded with pine and aspen, and watered by the rushing torrent of Boulder Creek. The camp was owned by Henry Lawrence, an old-timer of the West. Years ago, Lawrence had successfully prospected for tungsten in the nearby hills and had invested his money in tourist cabins.

Past seventy, he still enjoyed taking his campers for horse-back rides through the camp.

Our cabin had originally been used by gold prospectors who had come here even before Mr. Lawrence. It remained without any modern conveniences. Some of the other cabins had been fitted with electricity, but we used kerosene lamps and pumped our water from a mountain stream that seeped down from the snow fields fifty miles away. The stove in the tiny kitchen had a small reservoir which we filled with buckets of water and heated for shaving and cooking. The firewood was stacked behind the door, and we guarded it carefully against the damp weather.

On several occasions we took hiking excursions, climbing to the glaciers not far above our cabin. On our first trip we picnicked at noon in a pine and aspen grove on the mountain side, and by three o'clock we skirted a cliff and arrived at the timber line. I was fascinated by the queer, twisted little pine trees clutching the granite rocks at the timber line, defying the power of the winds that sought to root them up and cast them thousands of feet down into the gorges of the canyon. They reminded me of all rheumatic men, their joints painfully distorted by age and fever, gallantly holding fast to the last years that pervade the twilight of a lifetime. It was awe-inspiring to feel the deep, cold pressure of snow underfoot, while the sun shone hot and bright on my face. It would take ages to melt the snows; ages for the shrinking glaciers to shear the pinnacled tops from the mountain and level them into the hills below.

On another occasion, during our tour, we climbed the narrow paths which lead from Rainbow Lake toward the Isabelle Glacier. It required three hours of steady ascent to reach our destination, following a blaze of pointed arrows along the trail on trees and fallen logs. At the summit, cradled deep in its bed of rock, the frozen river lay, apparently immobile and quiet, although we knew it must be moving a few inches each day, a few yards each year in its inexorable journey downward to the sea. Along its wild, jagged edges was a deep crack just a few inches across; I tried to probe its depths with a long whip of pine, but there seemed no bottom. I had an eerie realization that not many human feet had desecrated the wild silence of this primitive region under the open sky.

On our way down to the timber line we ran into an electrical storm that was raging a mile high over the plains. The winds rose to hurricane proportions and we were forced to take shelter behind a rock which acted as a windbreak. Without warning, a bolt of lightning grounded on a nearby cliff and the earth shook under us. Our faces were stung by a shower of hailstones.

Within a half hour the weather had cleared and we were able to make our way back to our cabin.

The Rockies have a colorful history as mining country, and I came to appreciate a whole new aspect of the American past; as we explored, we found tungsten mines in various stages of desertion. We followed trails that led into the bowels of the earth to mining huts. One mine we visited seemed to have been deserted just yesterday, and yet it had not been worked for years. The machinery was practically intact; a glove lay on the forge. Bits of tools and metals lay everywhere; even the beams of the mine's damp roof were still solid. It was like walking through a lifeless world pregnant with memories.

The high point of my vacation was a visit to Central City, a ghost town tucked in the hills behind Switzerland Park. During its heyday as a mining camp Central was called the "richest square mile on earth."

As I walked down its streets and ran my fingers over the walls of mining shacks I seemed to be reliving a frenzied era of the past. Near the Teller Hotel I was shown the stone mill that once crushed out a stream of pure silver; and in the hotel lobby I felt the scales that had weighed out silver dust and nuggets. I ran my hands over a bullet hole in an old shop window that had been made by an outlaw's gun.

That night by the fireplace Miss Carpenter explained to me how Central City had begun. In 1857 Johnny Gregory, a penniless Southerner, hoboing through the Rockies, struck a vein of gold. The first pan of dirt yielded four dollars. Since then almost ninety million dollars' worth of gold has been removed from the vein. Prospectors poured into the region from all over America at news of the strike; a mining camp mushroomed into a city; shelters were slapped together virtually on top of one another along the steep sides of the gulches. No resident dared to spit out of his front door, "for fear of hitting his neighbor's chimney and putting out the fire."

As Central City's residents grew wealthy, public buildings sprang up that dazzled all visitors. The Teller Hotel became the Midwest's "Peacock Alley." The ladies who strolled in its lobbies wore gowns from Paris. Its dining room was furnished with Brussels carpets, lavish damask, a Knabe grand piano that had great mellowness of tone. An opera house was erected near Teller's that sparkled with beautiful frescoes and was lighted with a thousand gas jets hanging from the ceiling. The greatest actors and actresses of the times played on its stage when they toured the Middle West—Joseph Jefferson, Edwin Booth, Madame Janauschek.

Central City teemed with flamboyant characters who had been transformed from derelicts into millionaires with a lucky dip of the windlass. One immigrant who had recently come off the steerage from Ireland struck gold in Central City. Although he lived lavishly, he was unable to tell time to his dying day. Once when a friend met him in a café dangling a gold watch and chain, he teased the millionaire. "Hello, Pat, what time is it?"

Pat whipped out the watch, snapped open the cover, and held the face up to his friend.

"Sure and ye better be seein' for yerself. Ye wouldn't believe me if I told ye."

The miners were not exactly bluenoses. But Beelzebub finally met his match here. Father Machbeuf, a Catholic missionary, who had been assigned to the mining regions of the West, arrived at Central City and held his first Mass on the stage of Hadley Hall where the previous evening Rose Haided, the sweetheart of the sourdoughs, had performed to stamping feet. Father Machbeuf knew his miners thoroughly. After conducting Mass, he had the doors of the dance hall locked. "I know you are all anxious to be off to the gambling tables and get your glass of whisky," he announced. "However, none of you will be permitted to leave this room until you have given me enough money to build a church here." He nodded toward the collection box.

Father Machbeuf received enough money to erect a two-story house of worship.

Today Central City no longer produces gold. Its wealth has vanished; it has become a town of ruins some of which have been restored for tourists, antique hunters, collectors of Victorian furniture.

The Colorado timber line is gutted with ghost towns. We visited Caribou, twelve miles back in the mountains from Dream Canyon, approaching it up a hillside pocked with ruined mines, their mouths crumbled into heaps of rubble. The town itself had one solitary street; it ran uphill between two rows of houses with dilapidated walls so termite-eaten that a child could crush a stray timber in his hands. I felt an old hobnailed boot, as hard as iron, lying desolate in the afternoon sunlight. But at the foot of a hill, its roof gone and its interior purged by fire, stood an old school-house; its massive stone walls as sturdy as when they were built eighty years ago. The springs of mountain water that once served people are now used only by the cattle that come here with a herder for summer pasturing.

Hurricanes and massive winter snowstorms beat down with continual attrition upon the few cabins still standing at the timber line, and each spring finds another shelter or two sunk beneath the drifts. I explored several of those remaining, entering through sagging doors. I ran my hand over an armchair with cracked, moldy upholstery, discovered some old newspapers and bottles, several books with their pages glued together. Above the level of these cabins were others higher up the mountain, filled to their rooftops, inside and out, with snowdrifts. It was an uncanny feeling to pick a flower with one hand and make a snowball with the other.

We climbed higher to a point where the wind never stops blowing, looking for the old burying grounds of the town. On a tableland studded with aspen and pine, we found the broken fences, the toppled headstones of graves. One epitaph of an octogenarian especially interested me:

> Pause, Stranger, when you pass me by
> As you are now so once was I.
> As I am now so will you be.
> Prepare for Death and follow me.

Underneath, some passing wit had subsequently etched into the stone:

To follow you I'm not content
Until I see which way you went.

At the end of August we left Dream Canyon and started back for the East. The events of that month have remained indelibly with me.

The most important single happening and the one that culminated my efforts at Perkins was my graduation from the institution. This took place in June of 1945, when I was twenty.

Since March the class had been in a fever of planning—how were we going to raise the funds we needed for the senior prom? Eddie Murphy, my old classmate, was in his usual Irish mood for gaiety; "If we don't raise enough money now," he would tell me, "sure, and we'll nivver get out o' here with color."

"Drop the Irish, Eddie," I would say. "After all, you're a second-generation Irishman."

To collect funds for a gala prom the evening before graduation, our class hit upon the idea of establishing a small refreshment stand in an old coatroom off the corridor of the main building. Open twice a day—after lunch at noon and again at eight o'clock in the evening—it was a success from its inception. The balmy weather seemed to whet the students' thirst for soft drinks. During the first week in June, much to our pleasure, we discovered that we would have ample funds for the paraphernalia and trimmings of our final night at Perkins.

Selecting a class ring presented no difficulties; we chose a plain gold one with a symbol of the Perkins tower engraved on it. But there was interminable controversy regarding what clothes we were to wear. A small determined faction preferred ordinary summer dress; the rest of us wanted something more pretentious, so we decided on tuxedos with ruby-red studs and cuff links. Still, none of us could agree on what kind of jacket we were to wear. Tails were suggested and discarded; it would be too warm to put on black coats on a June evening. White jackets of linen took our fancy, since they were light and cool enough, but the dickering continued. Should the jackets be white or cream? Or should we wear the dark clothes after all, to be formal?

"Say, Murphy," I told Eddie one day, "why can't the other fellows make up their minds? Take the white coats, of course, even if they make us look like Pullman porters—those starched shirts are going to make it as hot as a griddle without putting on insulation."

Even after white coats were decided upon, our bickering was not ended; we still had not decided on the color of our class flower. Someone offered the suggestion that we use carnations but the rose triumphed. "They used the red rose last year," Murphy protested to me. "We want to be a little different this year. We should take a yellow or white rose." But red roses won out.

My family came up from Pittsburgh to attend commencement. The night of the prom was a windless evening, permeated with that peculiar softness that is characteristic of early summer. The air of the campus was fragrant with the heavy odor of opening flowers.

I felt awkward in the stiff white shirt and dinner jacket I was wearing for the first time. I kept reaching down again and again to feel the silk stripes that ran up and down my legs to see if they were still there.

Commencement was held the following noon. It was a hot day. We seniors again wore starched shirts. Perspiration trickled down my back as we started marching slowly up the aisle of Wright Hall and ascended the stage. Joe Jablonske was with me to interpret the ceremonies. He had always gone to morning chapel with me. This would be the last time we would sit together and share the familiar routine. The organ began to play and Joe told me to rise for the hymn. Then came the solemn invocation and a round of speeches by various dignitaries. I attempted to follow Joe's rapid summary of what the speakers were saying, but my mind drifted away. I tried to imagine what the other members of my class were thinking—Eddie Murphy, Fred Hayashi, George Winter. Was it the same thought that was puzzling me? Now that I had finished my work at Perkins, what about the future? There was no profit in worrying about the future. The Chinese have a proverb that says, "The journey of a thousand miles begins with a single step."

Chapter III

The I.H.B.

THE ANSWER to my immediate future was forthcoming shortly after my graduation from Perkins. Dr. Gabriel Farrell, the director, wrote a letter to Mr. Peter J. Salmon, Executive Director of the Industrial Home for the Blind in Brooklyn, New York, asking that I be admitted to the I.H.B. training courses.

A hundred years ago the vocational position of the blind in America was exceedingly insecure. If the blind were people of means, they could pursue a relatively normal life provided that they had the benefits of whatever educational programs were available to them. If they were not people of means, there was very little that they could do to enter upon a vocational career of any kind. Those with unusual intelligence, ingenuity, and imagination managed to carve a niche for themselves. Very few became outstanding.

In the 1880s a youngster of 17, Eben Porter Morford, lived with his parents in Clinton Hill, Brooklyn. The parents operated a livery stable. The boy had already begun to participate in it after school, on weekends and during the summer months. However, his career was abruptly cut short one evening when young Morford went into a corner drugstore to buy some drugs for his family. Some intoxicated youths were in the store, brandishing firearms. He heard one of them say, "I will see how near I can come to him without hitting him." Eben was looking at the store clock and thinking that he must hurry, for it was already five minutes to six, when he heard the sound of a pistol and felt a smashing blow across his face and temples. He was never to see again.

After months of medical care Morford was admitted to the New York Institute for the education of the blind. He stayed there for the next few years. Unable to follow his father's calling, he became a member of the Marcy Avenue Baptist Church, where he and several of his friends—some of them blind also—formed a social group, which they called the Mizpah Circle.

The Mizpahs made inquiries to see whether any organized effort had been made anywhere to change the pattern of life for blind people. They discovered that while something had been done on a limited basis in England and France, in Germany, Sweden and some of the other European countries, all of these programs were custodial in nature, offering care rather than rehabilitation.

It was not until 1893 that the group felt sure enough of its thinking to establish the first vocational service for the adult blind in the state of New York. It had taken some time to accumulate the few hundred dollars they felt was necessary.

On September 30, 1893, the Industrial Home for the Blind was opened. A small frame building on Lexington Avenue, Brooklyn, housed the first factory employing one blind man who began by caning chairs. There was a residence here, too, for working blind men who needed a place to live. By the end of the first year there were seventeen workers and residents.

In June of 1917 a young blind associate, Peter J. Salmon, joined the administration. He came out of Perkins institute to help with the sales and business program, which had grown considerably, including not only chair seating, but mattress making, broommaking and upholstery. The next ten years were ones of development and consolidation. Until the end of the Second World War Peter Salmon served as business manager of the I.H.B., becoming one of the nation's outstanding leaders in all phases of work with the blind. By the time he became executive director in 1945, he had completed blueprinting and projecting the I.H.B. of the future.

The authorities at Perkins were anxious that I commence vocational training at the I.H.B., but before leaving for Brooklyn I spent several weeks with my family in Pittsburgh. It was pleasant to be home again. My married sister Olga had two children. I enjoyed romping with my niece and nephew and telling them stories. I sat in the warm sun with them and repeated old fairy tales I remembered from my own childhood. Sometimes they would ask for a ghost story, and I would improvise: "Once upon a time there was a little girl named Mary who went to the store for a butter dish . . ." We would huddle together, and I would lower my voice, holding their attention till the very end.

My favorite child was my nephew, Don. He was a rolypoly little fellow who got into all sorts of mischief. When I slept late in the morning Don would come upstairs and climb into bed. Sitting down on my stomach, he would tickle my nose and pull my hair. I was compelled to dive under the blankets, pulling them about me for protection. Through them I could still feel Don romping about, searching for ways to reach me. I would pinch him through the thick wool and his screams would bring his mother to take him away.

One evening early in September my father and I took the train for New York. The eight-hour trip passed uneventfully. Lulled by the motion of the swaying coach, Father and I slept until it was nearly time to disembark in the early morning. This was the first time I had ever been to the Big Town, and I kept remembering all that I had read about it: the Empire State Building, the Statue of Liberty, the Cloisters.

We took a taxi that wove through the traffic, out across Brooklyn Bridge. Father kept swinging his head from side to side, watching the streets whizz by.

"These drivers, they go like crazy!"

Forty minutes passed. The taxi slowed down and finally stopped. We were at Gates Avenue. Miss Kitty O'Neil, Director of Social Service, greeted us in the lobby. She took us to meet Mr. George E. Keane, assistant to Mr. Salmon. I was surprised to learn that Mr. Keane was blind and had to use a hearing aid.

Upon leaving Mr. Keane's office, we met Mr. Peter Salmon, director of the Home. Mr. Salmon was to become one of my closest friends. There was a smile in his voice, and I was later to experience his keen sense of humor—a characteristic so typical of our Irish Americans. As I have said, Mr. Salmon himself is blind. I was to discover that several other I.H.B. executives were similarly handicapped. The I.H.B. was proving by the achievements of its own staff that handicapped men could be usefully employed.

Shortly after these introductions had been made the bell rang for lunch. While we were eating in the cafeteria of the Home, Father remarked, "There's a deaf-blind boy sitting next to you, Bob. Why don't you say something to him?"

I reached over, touched him on the arm. "Hello," I spelled into his hand. He took my wrist and raised my fingers to the level of his eyes, and I realized that he could see a little. "What is your name?"

"I am Oram Stone. What's yours?" He used the manual alphabet.

"Bob. Have you been here very long?"

"I came here last July. I work in the mats."

I was puzzled. "What do you mean 'in the mats'?"

"I make rubber mats. We turn them out in the workshops upstairs. I must hurry to get back to my bench. See you later."

Oram Stone, a husky young man in his middle twenties, was to be my roommate at the I.H.B. for the next two years. He had a faculty for asking innumerable questions. This habit was due to his narrow sphere of interests; he could not read Braille and he had no pastime to occupy himself with during the evenings. But he was vigorously earnest in his willingness to help other deaf-blind men with what little vision he retained. He had some hearing in the right ear and used a hearing aid, yet it seemed to be so slight that he got very little pleasure from it. I remember thinking that it was nearly the same type of hearing I had had while I was a child: just enough to hear the human voice if one spoke close enough to one's ear. Even then, words had to be repeated often, especially on days when Oram had a cold or the weather was damp.

Oram turned out to be one of the most guileless souls I have ever known. Because he lacked craftiness, he never lied or stole. If I happened to drop something in my room, Oram inevitably found it and returned it to me.

Once, after he had given me back a quarter, I asked curiously, "Why didn't you keep it?"

He seemed genuinely puzzled. "It's not my own."

"But you could spend it for something; no one would know."

"I don't need it. Why do you tell me to keep it?"

I had to give up the argument. Oram had that genuine moral sense which dictates to the saints.

After I had been living in the Home for a time, Oram suddenly lost his remaining hearing after a severe head cold. He was deeply depressed at not being able to understand what had happened to him.

"I can't hear," he kept repeating.

He possessed a small radio in his room, which had been adapted for the hard-of-hearing; it had an earpiece which could be plugged into the set. I often found him sitting in his chair, the earpiece in his hand, his eyes staring blankly at the radio.

"Can you make out anything, Oram?"

"Nothing. I am deaf."

He did the same thing with the old hearing aid he owned. Occasionally he would put it on, just to see if there was any faint sound that might give him hope. There never was, however.

Immediately upon joining the Home I began my training in the workshops. I learned to wind brooms, fold tape around heavy yarn, propel the cumbersome material under the swiftly moving needles of the electric Singer machine. It pleased me to take my place on the production line with the other workers, to feel the rhythm of the machines. This was during the final stages of World War II and most of the orders of our workshop came from government contracts. Our work had to meet the rigorous standards fixed for each product.

Even after the war, in any operation for which keen touch was primarily essential, our workers turned out products that stood excellently the competitive test in the general market.

One day Mr. Keane asked me to help in an experiment to determine the peak of production in our shop for the weaving of rubber mats. In a short time I passed the average; one day I made sixty-five mats in five hours. Mr. Keane called me into his office.

"My boy, you've done better than excellent. You've set a record for the shop."

During my first few months at the Home I never left the premises alone, because I lacked experience in traveling through unfamiliar, busy streets with a cane. I discovered, however, that many of the sightless men traveled about safely, and that even our deaf-blind men seemed unmoved by the danger in traveling alone. Some of our men did not reside in the Home but lived with their families, reporting daily to the workshops. I watched them coming to work each morning and leaving in the afternoon; it struck me as incredible that they could be so nonchalant about walking in the streets by themselves.

I became increasingly restless; I wanted to go by myself to the neighborhood stores when I needed anything, without having to ask someone else for help. But it was only when I mastered the use of a cane that I solved my problem.

The method is simple enough: the cane is a long, light, metal shaft that is swung from one side to the other so that it covers each foot as you move forward. The cane picks up curbs, obstacles, steps that run up or down, and anything else that may be in the path of the user. Properly employed, it provides safety in traveling about the streets and in unfamiliar buildings.

One winter afternoon I finally mustered enough courage to take up my cane and go outside alone, intending to stop at the corner grocery for fruits. As I left the Home I felt a sharp sense of misgiving. I barked my shin on an overturned barrel lying on the sidewalk. Side-stepping it, I ran squarely into an iron fence. Take it easy, I thought; you'll ruin your-self at this rate. I stood for a moment, rubbing my bruises. Then I moved ahead, more carefully this time, following a fence until I reached the corner. I turned right to where I knew the grocery stood. I was relieved when my hand found the large plate-glass window; it seemed so ridiculously easy.

Still, I had not yet tackled the real hurdle—that of crossing a street. I lingered over the idea a long time. Suppose, I thought, the person helping me across left me in the middle of the road? Or suppose the person helping me was not quite sober?

As I stood poised on the curbstone, tapping with my cane, I felt a tight feeling in the pit of my stomach. When some-one eventually took my arm, I stepped down from the curb rather unsteadily. But once across the street, I felt a revival of faith. Why, it had been as easy as pulling toffee! I walked along the unfamiliar stretch of pavement with my head high, shoulders back.

From then on, crossing the intersection held no terrors. But other sources of anxiety developed. I lived in a neighbor-hood that was a hard-bitten section of Brooklyn; the men of the I.H.B. seldom went out alone at night, fearing they might be attacked and robbed. There were occasions when I had to go out nights, however. Once I had a curious experi-ence. It happened on a winter evening, shortly after eleven o'clock. I discovered I had run out of aspirin so I decided to go to the corner drugstore. I went down to the street and walked to the corner, where I stopped and waited for some-one to help me across the intersection. A man came along and took my arm; we crossed together. I noticed that my companion had not left my side; I felt his hand feeling my pocket on the side nearest to him. I became tense, wondering what to do next.

"I can find my way from here, thanks." I tried to keep my voice calm. I moved the cane into my left hand so that I could free my right arm for action.

He refused to leave.

"Excuse me," I repeated loudly. "I'm going into the drugstore. I don't need any further help."

He must have sensed that I was aware of what he was trying to do. He moved his hand away from my side, where it had been tentatively groping for my wallet, and he slipped off.

I stayed in the store longer than was necessary, purchasing a bottle of lotion and a packet of cigarettes. Needless to say, I was relieved when nothing further occurred on the way home.

When a deaf-blind person travels alone, even in his own bailiwick, there are bound to be incidents he is unaware of unless someone relates them to him. I had gone out one noon on a personal errand. When I returned, I was met by Kitty O'Neil, our jovial director of social services. Kitty was laughing. "You made that Negro lady very angry with you."

"What lady?"

"The one who was trying to help you cross the street. I saw her from the steps."

"I didn't cross with a lady. It was a man; I noticed his overcoat."

"Well, a lady came up to you before the man and asked if you wanted to cross. You couldn't hear her. She really got mad! You stood like a statue while she shouted. She walked away in disgust before I could stop her and explain."

"Life can be beautiful." I felt a trifle sheepish. It must be disconcerting to shout at someone who never answers.

Once I had mastered the cane for local trips, the I.H.B. trained me to broaden my excursions. An instructor was assigned to teach the intricacies of foot travel. Eventually he decided I was ready to travel on the subway. I was given careful instructions beforehand.

"You'll be on your own today, Bob. I'll be trailing about fifty feet behind you. Now, what I want you to do is this: Walk to the Nostrand Avenue station, go down and find the turnstile. Then locate the platform at the bottom of the stairs."

He handed me several cards on which were printed instructions. "Wait on the platform until someone comes to you and offers help. Show him your first card, the one that says, 'Please help me onto the train to Queens Plaza.' When you're on the train show your second card to a passenger; it tells him to help you off at the Queens Plaza station. Then stay on the platform and tap your cane until you receive assistance. Your third card will get you on the Brooklyn train back to Nostrand; and while you're on it, show some passenger your fourth card, and he'll help you to get off at the right station."

I memorized the route thoroughly. In the afternoon we started out. I found the Nostrand Avenue station and went down to the turnstile. Everything seemed to go smoothly; a passer-by put me on the Plaza train, and another helped me off at my destination. Then the trouble began.

As I stood on the platform at the Plaza, waiting for the return train to Brooklyn, I held out the third card and tapped my cane. A man grabbed my arm. I was aware of the vibrating roar of an approaching train. The stranger pressed my sleeve and I followed him meekly into the subway car. Someone stood up and offered me a seat; I sat down beside the individual who had helped me aboard and reached into my pocket for my fourth and final card. I held it up for him to read. He made no response. I pointed to the card. Still no reply. The minutes passed. I became increasingly irritated. Suddenly the instructor who had been trailing me came rushing up.

"Bob, this is horrible! The man who helped you on the train is blind! He has a Seeing Eye dog with him."

I was aghast. "You mean he can't read my card?"

"No, and he's been talking to you and you couldn't hear him! He's getting angrier by the minute because you seemed so unfriendly after the help he had given you. Just let me explain it to him."

The instructor made it a point to stay with me until we got to the Nostrand Avenue station.

"Gosh, Bob, I was caught in a jam at the door of the train. I was fifty feet behind you. I thought I would lose you altogether when you sat down with the blind fellow."

He grunted, "This sort of thing only happens to you. You're the only one who gets himself into these queer predicaments."

"How so?"

"Remember the day you rolled the cat over with your cane? And the time when you ran into a truck parked on the sidewalk?"

"Be calm, Horatio—there are more things in heaven and earth than are dreamed of in your philosophy."

This curious incident caused quite a stir at the Home; everyone talked about it. It is not surprising that I have developed a fondness for the security of a taxi ride over a subway. Anyone who has been the victim of similar circumstances would.

I have traveled alone on railroad trains on several occasions and I have never seemed able to shake off the uneasy feeling that I would miss my destination. This fear is not entirely without basis; several times I have been helped out of a train that was just about to leave the station where I intended to stop. Being bundled about by porters and conductors alarms me. On one trip I missed New York completely by fifty minutes.

I had been visiting my old friend, Miss Carpenter, at her home in Waltham, Massachusetts. Upon the termination of my stay, Miss Carpenter and I loaded my luggage into a taxi and drove to the South Station. It was two in the afternoon when we reached the train platform.

"Now, remember, Miss Carpenter: please tell the conductor to help me off at New York."

"Don't worry, Bob, everything will be just fine."

Inside the coach I pushed the button under the arm rest of my seat, leaned back, and fell asleep. Five hours of traveling by rail, the coach swaying and singing, always rocked me into sleep. But it was only a fitful slumber; I kept rousing myself at every noticeable stop, feeling my watch.

At seven in the evening I noticed that the train was slowing down; the coach seemed to me to be running smoothly along a grading that was familiar, the final stretch of underground that leads to the Grand Central terminal. I slipped into my coat and prepared to leave.

Ten minutes later the train came to a halt. People went hurrying through the aisles; I had my hand resting on the side of my chair and counted each individual as he passed me. More than ever I was positive that I was in New York— but where was the conductor? Or the porter?

The long stop ended. The train began to move again, gathering momentum. I bolted upright in my chair and searched the wall panel until I found a push button. I pressed hard.

A porter came hurrying along. He touched my shoulder and I stood up, facing him.

"Porter, I thought that last station was New York; I was supposed to get off there. Here, write in my hand like this." I showed him how to trace block letters in my palm. But the fellow became agitated, pushed me back into my seat, and streaked away through the aisle.

"This is going to be dandy," I thought. "Maybe I'll land in St. Louis."

Soon a conductor was bending over me, shouting in my ear.

"Save your breath, conductor, I am deaf—I can't understand a word you're saying."

He shouted louder; I could feel the words bouncing from my ear like tennis balls.

"Here, since you won't write in my hand, please let me read your lips." I slipped my fingers along his face, but he brushed my hand aside and bellowed again.

Soon I felt him taking a pencil out of his breast pocket, then a pad of note paper. He scribbled something and held it up for me to read.

"No, no; I can't see it."

As I sat there, waiting for whatever chance might bring in the way of a solution, the train slanted downward and I smelled the faintly damp odor of a tunnel.

Eventually the train slowed down to a stop. The excited conductor came over to me, slammed my hat down on my head, grabbed me by the arm and led me off the coach.

A man took my hand.

"I can't hear. Please print in my hand—like this."

To my infinite relief, the fellow understood immediately. "Where are you going?"

"I was supposed to stop in New York. Where am I now?"

"You're in Newark, New Jersey. But we'll send you back by the next train."

He came back in a short time with another person who acted as my guide. I was ushered into a coach car with him. The train got under way. In thirty minutes I was back in New York, where my traveling companion hailed a taxi for me; he put me in it and dispatched me safely to the I.H.B.

During the early months of my stay a number of deaf-blind men joined the I.H.B. from various parts of the country. They came to be trained or to be served by one or another of the Home's various programs. The I.H.B. provided a special recreation room for the use of the deaf-blind, and here, in the evenings when our work was done, we gathered to discuss the events of the day. We varied greatly in intelligence and education, but virtually all of us had the voracious curiosity that sprang from our loss of hearing and sight.

I became friendly with Harry Weitman, a sociable fellow, gay and inquisitive; and Joe Klein, in his middle years, who was a mischievous, excitable sort. I got to know Orris Benson—whom we called "Grandaddy" because he was the oldest among us—and Arthur Hirschler, who sat quietly in a corner, continually smoking cigars.

Entering our cafeteria to eat, one noon, I noticed that Maude, our jolly Irish matron, was sitting at a table beside a young man whom I had never met before. Maude was feeding the stranger, and his arms moved up and down, as if he had the St. Vitus's dance. It puzzled me that anyone with a nervous disorder would be at the Home.

"Who is the new fellow, Maude?"

"He's a war veteran, Bob. His name is Harold Loughlin. Let me introduce you to him."

I shook hands with Harold. Since he wasn't able to communicate in any other way, I used lip reading.

The I.H.B.

"How long are you staying with us, Harold?"

"I don't know yet."

There are those who will say that deafness and blindness is the worst possible affliction; yet, curiously enough, I have never felt sorry for myself—only annoyed. Being in good physical health, I considered Harold's disorder combined with his blindness to be a more serious handicap.

Harold and I became close friends. In the evenings we sat in the smoking room and gossiped about everything under the sun; and on balmy nights in summer we climbed to the roof and sprawled out in deck chairs. It was some time before I found enough courage to satisfy my curiosity about his war experience. One evening, however, while we were at our usual exchange of small talk, I asked him.

"Harold, how did you lose your sight?"

"It happened as I landed on the beach at Normandy."

"Were you with the Infantry?"

"Yes, with the 4th Division. I was in one of the first battalions to disembark. When I arrived near the shore a shell exploded. I was knocked unconscious, and when I came to I couldn't see anything."

"And this affected your nerves?"

"Yes. The shell must have given me quite a wallop. I just woke up trembling—like this."

"Isn't there anything that the doctors can do to help you?"

"They tried everything they knew—all sorts of medicines and therapies. They even tried psychiatry. Something has snapped emotionally. For all purposes, I might as well be organically disabled."

All our deaf-blind men developed a genuine interest in Harold, even though he could only communicate through the printed alphabet, and his finger printing was impeded by his malady.

Harold stayed at the Home for nearly two years, then he went home to his family and set up his own small business, manufacturing toys, a trade he had learned in a veteran's hospital.

Several times a year Harold visits the Industrial Home, usually in the spring and around Christmas time. He has remained genuinely fond of the deaf-blind men. Harold's old tremor is still apparent, but it is more subdued. He appears healthier than he was while with us, and he seems happy to be making woolly toys for children.

Out of curiosity I once visited him in his shop in the Bay Ridge section of Brooklyn. I found him winding wool on wide frames. The walls were lined with shelves filled with toy cats, dogs, and teddy bears. The work table was piled with half-finished toys ready to be assembled. It was fascinating to watch Harold at work. The machine on which he wound the yarn hummed quietly; the noise apparently didn't disturb his nerves; indeed, his hands worked steadily. I could recall when loud noises had distracted him so that his hands would move up and down spasmodically.

"How is business, Harold? You seem to be an established firm."

"It's just fine. I can do all this work myself—except the trimming and sewing. Some of the children come in here after school and help me with that, and there are a few volunteers, too. I'm not going to be a Rockefeller, but I'm comfortable. I get orders from toy stores and department stores all over the East—just enough to keep me busy with work."

Harold has continued to exude a ruggedly cheerful attitude towards his handicaps. "You know," he told me recently, "I don't feel sorry for myself at all. It's you people who can't hear that I pity. You remember Don Lane, the hard-of-hearing fellow who stayed at the I.H.B. while I was there?"

"Yes, of course."

"Well, I ran into Don recently, and I invited him home for supper. When I introduced him to my sister he misunderstood what I said and thought it was my mother. 'I think you're wonderful-looking at your age,' he told her! Yes, Bob, God preserve me from ever becoming deaf!"

My leisure hours at the I.H.B. were taken up with various recreational activities. I played checkers with Joe Klein and some of the other deaf-blind men. Our checkerboards were made of cardboard, the positions marked out by square indentations into which both round and square pieces fitted. The small round and square men were easily distinguishable by touch; and when one reached the kings' row, the piece was turned over, exposing a small mark to signify that it was a king.

In Chinese checkers I was particularly successful, enjoying the speed and variability of the game.

While dominoes have lost their popularity with most people, I found it a relaxing game. I am not surprised that this was a favorite pastime of Queen Victoria and her Prince Consort, Albert. It is fascinating to move the counters into place, trying to block one's opponent's moves to gain the necessary points. I also became rather adept in rummy, twenty-one, draw and stud poker. I played penny-ante poker with cards marked by Braille symbols—the number of each card and the first letter of the suit were indicated at both ends. Whenever I played with seeing people, whoever happened to be beside me gave me the necessary information about openings, wild cards, bets, and raises as the game proceeded. I made my own decisions whether to stay or drop out, whether to raise or check, or to discard according to the hand I held. Except when the group was unusually large, I took my own turn as dealer, usually delivering the worst cards to myself.

One of the deaf men with very little sight of whom I became quite fond was Harry Weitman. Harry constantly spoke of his friends, Issy and Anna Stroh, who were both deaf. Several times Harry asked me to accompany him on a visit to the Strohs, but at first I refused. The sighted deaf use the sign language for the deaf, a means of communication which I had never been taught.

"Don't be afraid," Harry urged. "Issy and Anna will understand. They will be patient with you."

"But I'm very slow with the manual alphabet."

"You must try, always you must try." Harry had an odd, clipped way of speaking. "Please come with me—they will be very happy to meet you because you have a good education."

I fell back on the issue of transportation. "But we have to go by bus. We can't see or hear; how will we know when to get off at the right street?"

"Don't worry, I will give the driver a note to help us. And I have some light perception, you know. I can see little light from store on corner. Everything will be okay."

These arguments prevailed. One midwinter afternoon Harry and I dressed and went to the corner to wait for the bus. We waited only about ten minutes, and then the bus arrived. I followed my friend up the steps, paid my fare, and found an empty seat. I was filled with misgivings. Suppose we were to leave the bus at the wrong street?

I was relieved when the driver nudged my shoulder to signal that we had arrived at our stop. We climbed off the bus, crossed the street with a stranger, and Harry led me through an old section of Brooklyn until we turned in at an iron gate and found ourselves at the door of a small apartment building.

Isidor and Anna Stroh greeted me warmly. Issy, who had lost his hearing in childhood, was a stocky, jovial fellow with red hair. His wife Anna, a small, dark-complexioned, sunny-tempered woman, had been deaf from birth. She had two sons by a former husband; one was now a lieutenant in the Army. Issy and Anna were tiny in everything but their hearts; they were a perfect match for one another.

Issy and I soon gravitated to the subject of tools and electricity—interests which appealed to both of us. He brought out a copy of *Popular Mechanics*, a magazine that he had been collecting for years, and we turned the pages, discussing the articles and advertisements. All manners of things fascinated Issy. We talked of politics, boxing, New York and its restaurants, and even religion. Issy was helpful in explaining the Jewish religious rites to me. Though not orthodox in the conventional sense, he nevertheless displayed strong belief in the spiritual faith of his forefathers.

From our first meeting stemmed an unusual friendship. All of us—Isidor, Anna, Harry, and myself—enjoyed doing things together. Anna usually acted as Harry's guide and Isidor as mine. Though I was the youngest member of the group—the others were at least fifteen years older—the difference of age was no deterrent.

Issy was always eager to show me new things; his patience seemed inexhaustible. Twice a year we went to Coney Island, once on Memorial Day and again on Independence Day. I still remember a freak show we attended one hot Fourth of July evening.

We were walking along the boardwalk when Issy noticed a sign inviting visitors to "Come in and see some of the world's strangest attractions." My curiosity was aroused.

"I don't know if you will be able to see anything," Issy reported doubtfully. "It will probably be a stage show; they may not let us feel anything. But we can try."

We walked over to the ticket window. Issy bickered with the woman taking fees and we were finally admitted. A crowd was gathering in the big, barnlike room; at one end stood a stage about four feet high, and on either side were doors marked "Special Attractions."

"They're beginning now." Issy wormed his way closer to the stage. "I'll try to have them show you whatever is worth seeing."

The show began and Issy tried to describe it to me. A dwarf without hands came out and gave a demonstration of how he could shoot a revolver and put out the light of a candle, how he was able to shave and dress himself. He was followed by the "smallest woman in the world—twenty-two inches high, eighteen pounds." Then came a snake charmer and a three-legged man.

Though Issy tried to make his descriptions as vivid as possible, I became restless, moving about from one foot to another. Issy sensed my boredom. He began gesticulating violently to someone on the platform above us.

"They are going to let you feel the actors," he announced jubilantly. "It took me a long time to persuade them, but it worked."

I reached out to shake hands with the dwarf. Instead of hands, he had only small round balls at the ends of his arms, heavily calloused but extraordinarily mobile. The midget stepped forward, a dainty little doll, perfectly proportioned. Using lip reading, I asked her how old she was, and she replied in a high, shrill treble, "I'm twenty-two." I was enthralled by the tiny, dainty hands, the exquisiteness of the graceful figure, and the charming poise of the woman scarcely higher than a parasol.

"Look at this," Issy said excitedly. "Here comes the three-legged man. Just feel his legs, and then tell me if he's real."

I inspected the gentleman with the odd deformity carefully, but he appeared to be absolutely genuine. All three of his legs had the warmth of flesh and blood, and he could synchronize their movements marvelously. He even took a few clumsy dancing steps to show me how easily he could move about; the stage clattered with the sound of three shoes tapping in a slow jig. If I had thought to disclose him as a fraud, here was unquestionable evidence that he was truly one of the odd pranks of nature. And I was surprised to notice how gay he was. Surely, I thought, he must feel strange among so many normal people.

When the snake charmer approached, Issy drew back involuntarily.

"What's the matter?" I needled him. "Don't you like snakes?"

He made a sign of contempt. "I hate them. They're ugly."

"Nonsense, they're the cleanest of animals. Let me see this one."

I put out my hand until it touched one of the two coiled reptiles that encircled the dancer's neck. The body of the snake felt cool and clean; it was nearly as thick as my wrist, and it was perhaps eight feet long. It lay so quietly that I thought it was unreal until I felt its head sway a little and the darting movement of its tongue as it touched my palm.

"Feel it, Issy," I commanded. "It's harmless."

I tried to pull him forward, but he resisted. Then I thought of Harry. I reached over to pick up his hand, and moved it toward the snake, gently sliding his fingers along the swaying body. The hand was jerked away.

"What are you doing?" Issy wanted to know. "Do you think that was Harry?"

"Of course."

"Well, it wasn't. You had a stranger by the hand, and you nearly scared the life out of him!"

I turned around to apologize, completely deflated.

"Never mind now. He's gone." Issy chuckled. "He certainly took off in a hurry!"

Few people I have known possessed Issy's insatiable curiosity about things, despite his handicap. During the winter seasons we frequented the sports show at Madison Square Garden and the motorboat show at Kingsbridge Armory. Issy loved to show me things he thought would take my fancy. Even though a sign read "Don't touch," Issy managed to arrange things so I could feel the exhibits thoroughly. "I have a great deal of determination," he told me. "I will always find a way to show you anything you want to see."

On our frequent jaunts together through the Lower East Side of New York, where the merchants heap their wares in the open air, we browsed through countless fishing-tackle shops and hardware stores, and through the crowded aisles of the diamond marts.

"Here is the diamond center," Isidor once announced. "Would you like to go in and see some of the stones on display? There are beautiful diamonds in the windows—very beautiful."

"I don't think it would be reasonable. We aren't going to buy any jewelry for ourselves."

"Never mind, we can pretend."

Hesitantly I followed him into the diamond mart. But Isidor marched happily through the crowd, found a friendly face, and struck up a conversation. We were soon being shown diamonds, sapphires, opals.

Isidor, whose father had worked for years in the jewelry trade, had a genuine love for objects cast or made from precious metals. He loved design and beauty, and one of his fondest ambitions was to own a set of heavy, artistic flatware in sterling, decorated with an elaborate pattern.

"Silver is so beautiful," he would muse. "I love to see it— all white and gleaming under candlelight, surrounded by Limoges or Haviland china. But I'll probably never be rich. You're still young, so you can think of such things."

"Don't be so pessimistic," I chided gently. Isidor barely eked out a living working as a shipping clerk in a sweater factory. I've often wondered what he might have been if he could hear, if he had obtained a formal education. In his earlier years, after graduation from high school, he had wanted to study engineering, but he had been disqualified from entering any of the free city colleges because of his deafness.

"They wanted me to try a hearing aid, but I couldn't hear. Then they suggested an operation, but I didn't want to bother with that. The doctor told me that the tympanum bones in my ears are fused; I can hear sounds when they are loud enough, but I can't understand speech."

"Why didn't you risk the operation? It might have succeeded to some extent."

"Why bother? Besides, I don't think the doctors in those days were very skillful."

In spite of his failure to acquire a formal education, Issy had accumulated a wide knowledge of electricity, carpentry, mechanics. If Anna, his wife, complained about the television set or some other recalcitrant piece of equipment, he would repair it within a short time, his large, capable hands unerringly ferreting out the trouble.

Whenever an exhibition of sailing craft was held Issy made it a point to bring me along. At the motorboat shows he would wrangle with his customary vigor until the exhibitors would let us climb into the boats and look about. I loved to examine the neat, compact interiors; and on the larger cabin cruisers I was enchanted by the comfortable living rooms, dinettes, and sleeping quarters.

Issy insisted on my trying anything that was novel. During one visit to Madison Square Garden we came across a contraption called an Exercycle, a machine that supposedly provided the thrill of bicycling, rowing, and horseback riding rolled into one. I clambered onto the seat and the exhibitor pressed the switch. Up and down, forward and backward, I hurtled in a violent rocking style. My mouth fell open from shock, but I had to close it promptly because the strange motion made my teeth rattle like castanets. I was tossed about until I begged to get off.

"Now," I said to Issy, "it's your turn."

"No, thank you. I don't care for it. How did you like it?"

"You'll see soon enough." I gripped him by the waist and boosted him onto the seat. Then I threw the switch.

Up, down; backward and forward; the galloping motion of the device catapulted Issy until I broke into hysterical laughter. Issy waved his arm in the air. I knew he wanted to climb down, but I could not find the switch on the frenzied, bucking thing. Finally the exhibitor stopped it.

"How was it?" I inquired as soon as Issy was planted on firm earth.

"I told you I didn't care for it before I even sat on it. You never listen."

"Sorry, I really can't hear so well. And you looked so frightfully funny. How you shook!"

My active out-of-doors life helped me make an increasingly more efficient adjustment to the physical world. I became interested in deep-sea fishing in the fertile waters off Long Island. I was introduced to fishing casually enough. One afternoon, in the spring, Lou Bettica, an administrator in the deaf-blind department at the Home, asked me if I would like to join a group of blind people who were going fishing out of Sheepshead Bay.

"We're thinking of starting a club. No one has ever done this sort of thing previously, so we hope to be able to find out whether it is practical for our men. Wouldn't you like to come along? Mr. Keane will be going, too."

The thought of being aboard a real fishing craft, out on the open ocean, was too much of a temptation for me. I didn't care whether I fished or not; I was excited over the prospect of walking about a heaving deck and feeling the sting of salt against my face.

The day for the trip dawned with that peculiar balminess so characteristic of May. The boat we had chosen, *Amphion I*, was about forty feet long. I wandered about the deck and cabin, investigating everything that was new to me. When the engine throbbed into life I could feel the humming vibrations traveling along the whole deck. I climbed up the gently sloping planks until I stood as far forward in the bow as I could go; and as the motor gathered force and the craft slid away from the dock, I felt the exhilarating lift of the prow as it nosed into the bay.

Out in the channel we encountered the first rough water. Spume blew over the rail and struck me on the cheeks. The air was clean-smelling; the boat beneath my feet shook and trembled delightfully, dipping up and down, swaying and yawing from side to side—I loved it all.

We stopped to fish; the *Amphion* lay at anchor, with a gentle creaking sound of cable and wood. Someone gave me a hand line. I was determined to become adept at hooking a prowler, yet I soon discovered that fishing required more skill than I had anticipated. I took up my position next to Mr. Keane.

"Have you caught anything yet?"

"Yes, Bob, I've been catching quite a few right along."

"But *I* can't seem to feel any bites."

"Just keep moving your line up and down. They'll come soon enough."

I moved it up and down, up and down, until my arm ached with the unaccustomed exertion. Once I thought I had something on the end, but it proved to be someone else's sinker. Halfway through the afternoon I gave up the idea of fishing and stretched out on top of the cabin, glad for the warm sun. I was discouraged and disgusted. Never, I vowed, would I be seduced into a fishing trip again.

One of our deaf-blind men, Orris Benson, who was a charter member of the club, became an unshakable adherent of the sport. Orris continually came back with stories about the fish he had caught, about the rough sailing, the rain, and bluster that had prevailed during trips. I found his commentaries fascinating. Lou Bettica also added his brand of enticement.

"Do you know, Bob, Orris really enjoys this kind of thing. When he catches one he chuckles and smiles all over. And you should see him when he loses a fish! He bends over the rail and swears at it in the manual alphabet: 'Go, damn you, damn you!' It's wonderful to watch his expression."

The allurement was too powerful for me to resist in the

long run. I returned to the club and bought a light Shakespeare rod and a good reel.

"That rod of yours is too light for deep-sea fishing," Lou advised after we had returned from my second trip and I had caught nothing. "The tip bends too much; it doesn't have any backbone in it."

Following Lou's counsel, I purchased a bamboo pole. My skill began to improve; my fingers became more attuned to the light, quick strikes of porgies and sea bass. When the club was offered a free trip to Montauk at the tip of Long Island I was positive I would make a good haul.

For fishing addicts Montauk is a magic name; the sanctuary where the "big ones" flourish. During the warmer weather there are schools of tuna and swordfish, big fellows that tempt a sportsman's skill.

The journey by car from New York involved three hours of steady driving through the night. There were six of us in the car and space was limited. We were glad to stop, about six o'clock in the morning, at a small lunchroom just off the pier. The bacon and eggs and the scalding hot coffee tasted heavenly.

Once aboard the *Hacklehead*, I seemed to be unaccountably refreshed. Undoubtedly it was the freshness of the sea breeze rolling in from the ocean. Half an hour out of port we stopped in deep water; lines began tumbling overside into the water. Still an amateur, I found myself fumbling frantically with a pair of hooks, trying to splice them on to a line that tangled in my fingers. When I was finally ready I let my line freewheel into the spray, heaving a sigh of relief as I felt it moving downward.

This day the fish struck swiftly. I would drop the line down, and almost as soon as it touched the sandy bottom there would be a sharp "wham!" Quickly lifting the tip of my rod a few inches, I frequently had a fish on my line within seconds. At noon, when I laid my tackle aside and went to find my lunch, I had caught over forty squirming bass and porgies. My shoulder muscles ached with a gnawing twinge.

Lunch over, I took my place again near the bow of the boat. The fish were still coming in thick and fast, but I was tired; I decided to let my line dangle in the water. Suddenly I noticed that it was straightening, pulling outward and downward. I've let it out too far, I thought, and the current is dragging it along. I began to reel in. The line was heavy; I realized I had hooked into something large.

"Hello, Lou!" I called at the top of my lungs. "I've got a big one."

He came over, bent over the rail, peering down. He patted my shoulder with enthusiasm, but I couldn't release the tackle. I gritted my teeth, trying to suppress the pain that was steadily increasing with each turn of the reel.

Finally the net came over the side. There, thrashing slowly back and forth, was a large fish—the largest I had ever caught.

"It's a beauty," Lou said admiringly. "A hake."

A hake? I knew that hakes were solitary fish and that they rarely traveled in schools. What luck! I would win the boat pool!

Our club awarded pool money and other prizes for the biggest fish caught on outings and that year I really made a "killing." Besides winning two pools, at the annual banquet held at the clubhouse at the end of the season I won the door prize for holding a lucky ticket. Good fortune seemed to smile on me.

On several occasions I invited Issy and Anna Stroh to join us on a fishing trip.

The first time out Issy became distressed. He said his

stomach felt as though it were turning somersaults. He blamed the whole situation on "something" he had eaten for breakfast, but I realized it was a case of seasickness.

"Look at Anna," I pointed out. "She had the same breakfast, and she's catching fish like mad."

"I'll be all right soon." He slouched against the cabin bulkhead. "Just let me rest, please."

I knew that staying in the cabin would only prolong the illness, so I persuaded him to climb to the deck, where there was fresh air and sun.

After the trip was over we went back to the Strohs' home for dinner—and what a dinner Anna cooked! It rounded out this and subsequent fishing excursions. She prepared fish rolled in cracker meal, salt, and pepper and egg. Whether it happened to be fluke, blackfish, porgies, or sea bass, she never failed to delight our palates, famished as we were from long hours of exercise in the air.

The most memorable of all the fishing trips I participated in began quietly enough. One calm, cloudy October morning, we sailed out, twenty-five of us, aboard a thirty-eight-foot boat called the *Phil Jr.*, skippered by Buster Brimlow. It wasn't a particularly good trip, as far as fishing went. Only a few porgies were caught. Much to our dismay, there seemed to be millions of burgalls about. Burgalls are inferior fish that steal bait from hooks. They are small, lithe, and have rows of sharp spines along their sides.

We were relieved when late in the afternoon the bell sounded for our return to the bay. The motor started, muttered a bit, and then died. I turned to Harry Weitman who was fishing beside me. "It looks as though we are having a little difficulty."

The engine started once more, turning over with a raucous whirl that subsided and picked up again. Curious, I called for

Lou Bettica, who had been fishing from the after part of the craft. "What's the matter? Are we having engine trouble, Lou?"

"We don't know yet, but I don't think it's serious. We'll be under way in a few minutes. Get your tackle packed."

The minutes lengthened into half an hour of waiting. Then Lou came forward again. "Buster, the captain, says that there is to be no smoking now. He's working on the motor, and he's afraid the fumes will be dangerous. Tell Harry and Enio."

When I relayed this message to the other two deaf-blind men on board, they seemed disinterested. Harry's reaction was to sit down on the top of the cabin, fill his pipe, and start smoking. Enio, who had a wife, merely complained that he would miss supper and Etta would worry.

"Put your pipe out," I told Harry. "No smoking; Buster is trying to fix the engine."

"How long will we stay?"

"I have no idea."

The boat rocked back and forth, heaving with the swell of the incoming tide. We waited patiently, but now that the fishing was over we were more than ever aware of the uncomfortable autumn chill.

Lou came back to us. "Move to the back; the rail is weakening up here and Buster is afraid it will break loose. No, don't bring your kits—just leave them where they are."

We moved to the afterdeck, where the captain had set up folding chairs. Men were sitting about, talking quietly. We took it for granted that Buster would finish his repairs within a reasonably short time, and we would head back to shore.

"It takes long time—too long," Harry complained after we had spent an hour in desultory conversation. "It is very bad. I am uneasy. Do you think maybe we will be here longer?"

"Don't worry."

"Does boat have radio?"

"No."

"If real trouble is coming, how will we go home?"

"Swim."

"Don't be crazy—it is miles. Ask Louis."

I called Louis and asked him how long he thought we would be stranded.

"No one knows. Buster has just signaled a message about us to the Coast Guard. We can't do much except wait now."

"But what about the motor; can't he repair it?"

"Something went wrong with the flywheel—it won't mesh. We'll have to sit here until the Coast Guard cutters come to pick us up."

Seven o'clock came and went; at eight o'clock it was dusk. Harry, able to see a little, muttered, "No good. I fear we are in bad place. I hope Coast Guard coming soon."

As a matter of fact, under continual exposure to the damp chill of the water and night, all our tempers were becoming frazzled. Petty differences were magnified; the atmosphere was charged with tension.

After ten o'clock I turned to Lou and asked, "Can you pick out anything—lights or boats?"

"No, I never saw such blackness in my life!" Lou wagged his head unhappily. "What will my wife think?"

Tired and hungry, I decided to go down into the cabin. All the seats were taken; men were sitting, their legs sprawled awkwardly in every direction, exhausted by the long waiting.

Time passed, the darkness grew deeper. The *Phil Jr.* dipped and yawed in a graceful little minuet. Whenever there was a more decided lurch the folding chairs rolled from side to side. I kept trying to balance myself against the sudden tilting of the deck whenever we hit a stronger squall, but it was no use. Several times I fell against Arthur Croft, a blind friend who sat next to me.

Finding a thick coil of rope in a corner, I sat down on it with my head resting on one side of the loop. Soon I fell sound asleep.

When I awoke I felt my watch. Midnight. We had been at sea for sixteen hours. I climbed the ladder to the deck.

Buster came over to me. "This is rough. How do you feel?"

"Not bad, you know."

He patted my shoulder, and I felt him turn to scan the darkness. I sat down on a life preserver and lit a cigarette.

I had just finished smoking when Buster pounded me on the back. The others, sleepy and cold, sat up in a sudden vigilance.

"The Coast Guard cutter is coming!" Lou announced jubilantly. "We can see the searchlights."

Buster and a helper climbed to the bow and threw a rope to the waiting cutter. After a brief interchange of comments, the larger boat swung in behind us and began pushing us along. The *Phil Jr.* bobbed slowly, dancing from side to side.

"I can see searchlight," Harry said, pointing above us. "It is very big and bright! First right side, then left side—pushing us."

As the bow cut crookedly through the water, a fine spray came showering back over the deck like a cold, penetrating autumn rain. No one was talking now. Harry leaned against the cabin bulkhead, hugging his knees, his chin resting on his forearm; Enio sat cross-legged like a Buddha, his hands folded in his lap. Only Louis and a few other men with partial sight kept shuttling back and forth across the bobbing deck.

The I.H.B.

The journey back to the bay was a long one. It was not until after three in the morning that we entered the channel that led to the piers. Another big Coast Guard cutter, waiting outside the channel, came alongside. Between the two big boats we were slowly shepherded into berth.

It was wonderful to feel once more the soil underfoot. At the gates a small group of people were waiting to meet us.

Vincent Smith, an associate living at the Home, came over and shook my hand.

"I'm glad to see you and Harry and Enio safely home."

"You can't imagine how happy we are."

"Would you like some coffee?"

"Nothing better."

The hot coffee revived us. We climbed into a waiting car and headed back to Gates Avenue. It was nearly five o'clock when we arrived home. Wearily I climbed up the stairs to my room, threw off my excess clothing, and dropped my pack on the floor. I decided to stay up until breakfast was served at seven. As I started down to the dining room I stopped at a window and put out my hand to test the weather. The wind was rising and rain was falling heavily. We had just managed to beat the storm home.

None of us who had been marooned that night has forgotten the experience. But the classic reaction was the remark of old Zelig Tepper, which made the rounds for weeks afterward. Zelig was a member of our fishing club; during the trip he had lost his rod and reel when they had fallen overboard during a sudden lurching of the boat. As we came into port somebody asked Tepper if he was glad to be safe and sound on dry land, and he replied, "With my great loss, what can it matter?"

Chapter IV

"I Sense Her Presence Everywhere"

FROM THE moment I had entered the Industrial Home for the Blind in September 1945 to learn a trade so that I would be able to work for a living, I had considered such training to be only a stop along the way. For years I had insisted to my family that I would someday enter college. Only one deaf-blind person had succeeded in accomplishing this— Helen Keller, fifty years previously. And she had been trained from childhood by a companion-teacher. The general lot of the deaf-blind was to spend their lives in obscure manual labor.

Nevertheless, I had frequently discussed with my mother the possibility of a college education and a professional career, always with the conviction that it would come to pass. We spoke of other handicapped people who had broken out from their imprisonment—Senator Dunn, a blind man prominent in the politics of Pennsylvania. We talked of Helen Keller, herself, a legend to millions.

The staff of the Industrial Home was aware of my ambition, and one afternoon when I had been at the I.H.B. for less than a year, George Keane, who had first put me to work in the shops and had been keeping an eye on my training, called me into his office. "Bob, we have given you every standard psychology test available. We believe it may be possible for you to compete on a college level with seeing and hearing students."

Blind himself since his teens, Mr. Keane had gone through Columbia University and had taken his law degree at St. John's University. It was heartening to realize Mr. Keane had confidence in my ability to undertake such an uncertain project.

The first step was to find a college near home. Mr. Salmon, our director, sounded out the authorities of St. John's University in Brooklyn. Father Mahoney, the president, and Dean Meyer of St. John's College were frankly skeptical. The odds against my success seemed great. But they decided to give me a chance.

The I.H.B. staff made thorough preparation, aware that if I failed it would be all the more difficult for others like me to find places in institutions of higher learning. Much more was at stake than the success or failure of an individual. The New York State Vocational Rehabilitation Service readily agreed to contribute scholarship money toward the defrayment of my expenses. In addition, the American Foundation for the Blind made a very substantial annual scholarship available to me. The Howe Memorial Foundation of Boston, which had been interested in my early education, also agreed to contribute to my first year at school. The I.H.B. met the balance of the costs.

A search was instituted for a student-companion who would accompany me to classes, spell out the lectures into my hand in the manual alphabet, and translate written notes and lessons into Braille.

On July 5 Mr. Keane called me into his office and notified me that they had found their man, a high-school graduate who was willing to undergo the necessary intensive training. Without any preliminaries, I was introduced to Johnny Spainer, who was destined to spend the next nine years with me as my guide and my friend.

"Bob"—I detected the brief acrid odor of a match as Mr. Keane lit his cigarette—"you'll have to begin right away teaching Johnny all he will need to know before the college opens in September. Since you'll be working in the shops during the day, keeping up with your vocational training, both of you will have to arrange your schedules so that you can be together during the evenings."

That night in my room Johnny and I began our studies together. John was obviously uneasy, and I was strangely hesitant myself in the presence of this young man who had been chosen to be my eyes and ears in the curious new adventure that awaited me. Johnny followed my instructions in a quiet, steady way. I began by teaching him the letters in the manual alphabet. He learned the entire system in a couple of hours and, even though he frequently confused his letters, he showed definite promise of soon acquiring speed with them. He formed perfectly clear speech with his long, flexible fingers.

Toward nine o'clock, feeling tired from my exertions, I said to Johnny, "Let's go out for a walk; it would be a good treat to have a soda somewhere. You're probably as tired as I am, and I don't think we should push our luck this evening."

"Okay," he answered, stumbling a little as he spelled out this answer slowly.

Down on the street a little breeze had sprung up from the overheated pavements. As we came to the park we could smell the dew on the dusty green leaves, and the cool spray of the fountains spilling under the trees. We sat on one of the benches and relaxed.

"You know," I commented, "you needn't grip my arm tightly while we are walking in the street. Just pretend I'm not with you and walk as you ordinarily do. When we come to a crossing, pause just a moment, so I'll know there's a curb there. Otherwise, forget I'm along."

I was to discover that Johnny had to be drawn out slowly. He was shy and incapable of communicating freely because of a strong reserve. He gave his trust only gradually.

This first evening of our acquaintance, indeed, in all the years that I was to know him, I never witnessed an emotional outburst from him. And yet when I came to understand Johnny I found him utterly dependable and compassionate as a friend. Tonight I found myself wondering what manner of boy my new friend was. Would he mind spending his time studying the alphabet with me while other fellows were out on the ball field or strolling through the park with their girl friends? What ambitions did he have for himself after he graduated from college? He was unusually taciturn for a youngster of seventeen.

Only a week after our introduction I was amazed to find him using the manual alphabet fluently.

"How on earth did you ever learn to spell so quickly?"

"I've been practicing words while reading the newspaper, Bob. Also whenever I find myself humming a popular song, I spell out the words into my palm manually. People must think I'm crazy, moving my fingers against my palm while I sit in a streetcar or walk down the street. But the best way to learn the manual is to live it."

However, learning to read and write Braille proved to be a much harder task than mastering the alphabet, especially when we began grappling with the complex signs of contractions and abbreviations in advanced Braille. I admired Johnny's determination to succeed. He never complained, never showed the slightest impatience. Though he made numerous errors, he was willing to repeat reading entire pages when I insisted he must be accurate.

That was a summer neither of us shall forget. My schedule was crammed full. After finishing my day's matmaking in the I.H.B. shop I would change my clothes and hurry over to my room to supervise John's exercises. There was an endless stream of paper work, scores of mistakes to correct. And there was the fear, continually haunting me, that Johnny would not become sufficiently expert in Braille in time for the opening of college.

At times the whole project seemed grotesque to me. I would awake nights in a sweat and suddenly wonder what I was letting myself in for. I knew that college would not be like any other school I had attended; there would be unfamiliar subjects, frequent testing, and a much more accelerated tempo of studying. I was beset with a variety of doubts. How would I be able to find material for research when I was expected to write essays? Would my new companion be attentive during lectures and would he be able to transmit lectures and classroom discussions accurately and swiftly enough into my hand?

However, the problem that concerned me above all was having all the textbooks I would need for my courses transcribed into Braille. The Home undertook to tackle this problem with characteristic vigor, contacting members of the St. John's faculty to find out what courses I would be required to take the first year.

The very titles of the books I needed awed me—textbooks on dialectics, apologetics, essentials in English expression. When titles of the books required for the freshman year were received by the Home, Vincent Bettica, the brother of Lou Bettica and our director of the deaf-blind department, contacted groups of volunteer Braille transcribers around the country. Among those approached were the Braille Club of America, the Plymouth Church of the Pilgrims Braille Press, the New York Guild for the Jewish Blind, the Brooklyn Braille Center, the National Braille Press, and scores of housewife volunteers who were expert in transcribing the printed page into its Braille equivalent as a community service, and who willingly accepted the task of translating my textbooks. They did it in groups; each individual worked on about fifty pages of text—three or four women to a volume.

To give some idea of the extent of the task these generous souls undertook for me—twelve bulky volumes of Braille were required for the translation of a single textbook in philosophy; my history of theology consisted of seven Braille volumes. A single textbook in English literature had to be farmed out to twenty transcribers.

It was a laborious task, translating these books, and as the date of the opening of college grew near and the bulk of my books had not arrived, my anxiety became almost unbearable. I was somewhat appeased when my Braille edition of Webster's unabridged dictionary showed up. There was something comforting about having thirty-two volumes of Braille in my possession.

In addition to my worries over books I needed a typewriter which I could use in class and during tests without disturbing the other students.

"I thought you already owned a typewriter," Mr. Keane said.

"I have an old Underwood portable, but I'm afraid it will distract the other students. It makes a frightful racket."

"What kind of machine would you need?"

"I don't really know. Someone told me about the Underwood noiseless; it's a new model and supposed to be very quiet. Do you think we could get one?"

"I think the American Foundation for the Blind has a few of those machines on hand, Bob, but they are pretty expensive. Let me call them up; I'll let you know in a day or two what we can expect."

When my new typewriter arrived I was more than delighted. It was quiet and dependable, and I felt that it was the perfect answer to the problem of taking tests, although I was not at all familiar with the procedures used in college.

Eventually my textbooks trickled in, but in an assortment of conditions. Some were sent back to us in permanent bindings; others in loose-leaf bindings; some shellacked and others unvarnished. In some instances the Home had to assemble batches of pages submitted in sections from various parts of the country, literally hours before I was about to go into the classroom.

However, the job was done and done magnificently, considering the circumstances. I will be eternally grateful to the scores of volunteers who made my going to college possible.

One day in early September, Mr. Salmon called John and me into his office. "Bob, how would you like to meet Helen Keller? I thought it would be nice if you could have a little get-together. Perhaps she can give you some good advice about her own experiences in college."

"That would be wonderful!" I didn't try to conceal my excitement.

"Well, I'll do my best to arrange a meeting shortly."

Back in the room where we were studying the mysteries of Braille, neither John nor I seemed interested in our usual course of practice. Instead we sat beside the desk and talked of Helen Keller.

"Mr. Salmon told me that he has known Helen Keller for years," John volunteered. "Since they are old friends, you can feel pretty certain we'll have a get-together soon."

"I've always wanted to meet her—ever since I was a child. My parents talked about her, and of course I've read her book, *The Story of My Life*. Have you ever seen her, John?"

"Not in real life. But I've seen her picture in the newspapers and magazines."

Several days later, after our first feeling of excitement had died away under the influence of routine, Mr. Keane had further news. "Mr. Salmon has arranged for you and John to meet Helen Keller in New York tomorrow. Johnny can pick you up after lunch. Then you can both be at her hotel by one o'clock. Mr. Salmon will be waiting for you in the lobby and will make the introductions. And it might be a good idea to take her a small corsage of roses, too. Helen is very fond of flowers."

"I'll ask John to stop at a florist's on the way in."

John and I dressed in our best suits for the special occasion. On the way to the hotel, stopping at a little florist's shop on Broadway, we picked up a handsome corsage of rosebuds, half open and exhaling the delicate fragrance of Indian summer.

We were met in the lobby by Mr. Salmon, who took us immediately to a room that had been set aside for our use. We waited only a few minutes. Then Mr. Salmon came back and said to me, "Helen will be here in a moment. She is really excited about this meeting."

John stood up. "Here they are now," he told me, spelling as swiftly as he could.

Miss Keller took my hand in her own. I remember vividly how warm, how energetic, her handclasp was. She was then in her sixty-fifth year, but no one would have guessed it if he had merely taken her hand. Her eager clasp conveyed all that youthful vigor which has characterized her personality and set aside the weight of years.

"I think it's wonderful that you are going to college, Bob," she said. "It has been nearly half a century since I graduated from Radcliffe, and times have changed so much since then. You have courage to begin a project like this."

She paused and her fingers lay quietly for a moment in my hand. "You will have many difficult situations to face. God knows the trials you will have to endure. But you will succeed, I am sure of it. You will overcome all the difficulties if you really believe in yourself."

As she spoke so quietly and confidently about the certainty of my success, I wished just for this once that I could have been able to see her face brighten up with that smile that had become so well known everywhere.

Suddenly, as I sat there, the words of someone else who believed in me with the same quiet assurance of Helen Keller returned to my mind. "You must never give up hope of going to college and becoming a writer, Bob." It was the last thing Professor Dana had said to me before I graduated from Perkins.

Here were two people who believed implicitly that I could do the job. One of them had done it herself and had waited half a century for another to follow in her footsteps. And now she clasped my hand as if to pass on to me the victory.

As we rode home in a cab from our meeting, I kept picturing in my mind this magnetic woman whose career had been a lodestar of my own. I would not disappoint her hopes in me.

The day for our matriculation came before John and I quite realized that summer was over, that eight long months of study lay ahead of us. Yet I recall that particular Tuesday with a feeling of relief. Going to college to register meant the end of months of anxious waiting; now we could begin in earnest what formerly had been only planning and conjecturing.

St. John's College, founded in 1870 by the Vincentian Fathers—followers of Saint Vincent de Paul, the Apostle of Charity—as a major institution of higher learning in America, is permeated with the mellow atmosphere of a school that has sunk its spiritual roots deep into the past; it has the old floors that creak under the weight of hurrying feet, the paneled rooms with scarred desks; and, above all, the indefinable quality of sturdiness and stubbornness that is usually found in old buildings.

My first day of school was unexciting. The freshmen assembled in the gymnasium. One speech by a faculty member followed another. John, striving to keep pace with the exercises of matriculation, quickly suffered the strain of using the manual alphabet continuously. He complained of stiffness in his wrist and frequently shook his hand loosely to free his muscles from their tenseness. As the first hour dragged by, I, too, began to weary of the sustained concentration of reading what John was transmitting.

Sitting for several hours while people whom one can neither see nor hear are delivering wordy speeches is a severe test of the deaf-blind person's ability to stay awake. Eventually my drowsiness was overwhelming. "I think I'm going to fall asleep."

"Better not," John warned. "Some of the good Fathers may be watching us. And don't speak so loudly—everyone will hear you. Use the manual alphabet, but use it slowly so I can follow it."

I heaved a sigh and leaned back in my seat, making myself as comfortable as I possibly could on the hard folding chair. I drifted into sleep.

John shook me back into consciousness. I found him quivering with laughter.

"You looked so innocent, Bob. All your features were relaxed. But for heaven's sake, keep awake; the priests look at us every so often."

By a valiant effort I pulled myself together; I wriggled my toes until I felt reasonably wide awake.

"How much longer will it last?"

"It's nearly three o'clock now. The priest has just announced we'll be going over to the chapel shortly for benediction."

When the assembly was dismissed we hurried across to the church, mingling with the crowd of other students. The fresh air had a crisp, bracing quality so common to September weather. "Johnny, the boys and the professors here are going to have to get used to the idea that two boys are studying as a single student. Did we create any stir as we sat together in the gymnasium? Did anyone notice us using the manual alphabet?"

"I don't think so—at least they never showed it. We held our hands so low that probably no one could see us using it."

"Here's the church." I detected the fragrance of burning incense as we climbed the stone steps leading into the church of St. John's. Johnny pressed my hand for silence and we threaded our way through the crowded aisle to a seat near the altar.

I dropped to my knees, and all at once memories crowded into my mind. From the onset of my boyhood illness my mother and Dad had placed their trust in God that I would not be stranded in my night.

Shortly after my illness Mother had taught me a little prayer to Saint Gabriel that I recited every night before I went to bed. I remembered how my father, on his way home from the steel mill, had visited the Monastery of the Little Flower of Jesus each week to pray for me, and how he had brought back a tiny vial of blessed chrism which Mother applied to my eyes and ears before she tucked me into bed. Only gradually had I come to realize how much hope rested on that tiny vial—how many whispered prayers accompanied those drops that fell so softly into my sleepy eyes. . . .

And now I was kneeling in the chapel of St. John's, prepared to take up a college career under the guidance of my Heavenly Father. He had brought me this far in His Mercy. He had answered the pleadings of a humble steel worker and his wife.

"Our Father Who Art in Heaven . . . Hallowed Be Thy Name . . ."

Johnny and I left the church in silence. We passed through the college gate and turned our steps homeward. Johnny spelled into my hand, "I hear you mumbling—what are you saying?"

"Mumbling? I really don't know how to describe what I feel today. I guess I was still praying."

Gradually Johnny and I settled into the college routine. We attended classes five days a week. In addition to transmitting classroom discussions, Johnny took notes for both of us and Brailled mine for me after class. During lectures Johnny sat on my left and spelled into my hand. Having had only two months of training in the manual when college opened, he was able to cover only about half of what the professor was saying. But as he gathered speed, more facts were communicated to me. Frequently a professor would stop to write on the blackboard, and Johnny would take the opportunity to round out his transmission. After classes I poured over my bulky Braille books, struggling to memorize the facts.

We took five courses the freshman year—economics, American history, religion, moral guidance, and logic. Problems cropped up suddenly. In economics, for instance, the class launched at the outset into a study of supply and demand. I was astounded to discover that the textbook had suddenly been changed and the book that had been Brailled for me was not to be used. However, the professor, upon hearing of my dilemma, permitted me to continue to use my text.

However, it was not easy for me to adjust to my studies. Time and again I was tempted to give up and return to the safe, known things.

There were numerous disheartening incidents. I typed my term papers, and Johnny Spainer would go over them for typographical errors. One night I excused myself from a social evening with Johnny and friends and went into my room to type out a history paper. I spent four hours at the job. When I emerged I handed my sheets to Johnny, breathing a sigh of relief. "It was worth giving up my social evening to get this paper done." Johnny didn't have the heart to reply. Later I learned that my sheets of paper were totally blank. I had taken out my ribbon when I had cleaned the typewriter that morning and I had forgotten to replace it.

There were wryly humorous incidents, too. One day as Johnny and I walked through the college gate conversing as usual by holding hands, one witness who had not heard about me, came rushing into the dean's office and reported to him a flagrant exhibition—two male students sauntering along the street holding hands.

Usually I carried several volumes with me when I attended classes. Since Braille is bulky, these books were ordinarily concerned with courses which I was studying. But there were times when I felt sufficiently erudite to do without textbooks. On such occasions I'd slip a volume of poetry or part of a recent novel under my arm and surreptitiously read it in the classroom.

During one class Father Brown, my professor of philosophy, discovered my departure from the rigid road of study. We were reviewing the lives of prominent philosophers. After the first fifteen minutes of lecturing I signed to Johnny that I was going to read; I settled myself in a comfortable posture, picked up a detective story, and became deeply engrossed in the underworld of crime. Suddenly John tapped my arm.

"Father Brown wants to know what you're reading. He says you look very contented, just like a Cheshire cat."

"It's nothing special," I answered evasively.

"Don't tell me. Tell Father Brown—he's waiting."

"It's nothing very interesting," I said loudly, so that my voice would carry to the rostrum. "Just a book, that's all."

"He wants to see it. Hand it up to him."

I felt uncomfortable. Still, there was nothing else I could do. I handed the book to the waiting priest.

After glancing at the title, Father Brown stepped down from his dais and came over to me. I put up my hand to read his lips. He was smiling broadly.

"So you're reading a murder story here?" he said, trying to keep a straight face and making a poor show of it. "Why aren't you studying your philosophy?"

"I already know how the life of Spinoza turns out, Father; but I don't know how this detective story will end." I felt acutely embarrassed, knowing that the other fellows in class were watching us.

"Well, let's put this book away for the rest of the class, young fellow. I'll expect you to follow the lecture or read a few chapters from the textbook you have with you. If you need something to occupy your time, I can give you an essay to write."

"Don't bother about the essay, Father."

He chuckled and climbed back to his desk. For the rest of the period I kept the book closed, making a show of indicating particular interest in what Father Brown was saying. Johnny reported with his fingers: "You should have heard the fellows howl when Brown caught up with you. They really enjoyed it."

"Of course they would. I guess I'm no angel after all."

"You never were an angel to begin with."

For my first mid-term examinations, which were to provide the first real test of my ability to stay on at St. John's, my studying became frenzied. Nightly for a week previous to the exams, I sat up, huddled in the corner of a sofa, memorizing thick bundles of notes and verifying them by reading the books I had on hand. Burning the midnight oil is an understatement; I would burn away the whole night without sleep. I studied in half-hour periods; then I would sit still, holding my head in one hand while I tapped off the information I needed with the fingers of the other. Blessed with a reasonably good memory, and depending upon repetition, I was able in most cases to memorize the material almost verbatim.

In the early morning, I would hurry down to breakfast, still clutching the bundle of notes I was studying under my arm. I would scan them all over again, eating with one hand and reading the mass of pages with the other under the table.

When John arrived at eight-thirty I'd ask: "Did you sleep last night?"

"For a few hours. I was studying those notes on dialectics until three o'clock. My mother had to haul me out of bed this morning."

"And I stayed awake all night. Did you see that column of twenty essentials of supply and demand in the economics notes? I can only remember fifteen; the others keep slipping out of my mind like eels."

"You don't have to remember all of them. Just remember enough to pass."

"How do you know which ones the prof is going to ask about, wise one?"

"Let's not argue; it's time to be off to school."

In the cafeteria with fifteen or twenty minutes to spare before the second bell rang for class, we sipped coffee and compared notes.

"Let's look at those notes on dialectics," I suggested. "Have you memorized the essential parts of the syllogism?"

"Major, minor, and conclusion."

"Bravo! John. You're a seven-day wonder. Let's drop it all for a while; my head is in a spindrift. What I need is another cup of coffee and a little time to collect my thoughts. I keep wondering whether, at the last moment, most of the material will vanish like smoke."

It had been decided that Vincent Bettica, the brother of Lou Bettica, would accompany me to class on the day of the examinations and transmit the test papers in the manual alphabet.

When we reached the classroom for the first exam in apologetics Vincent went to the proctor to receive the test. When he returned to me I extended my hand to feel the number of pages, as if this would somehow convey an idea of the difficulty of the test. Just before I sat down at the typewriter, I clasped my hands together in a moment of prayer. Vincent offered a prayer, too. Then we settled down to the exam. As I perceived Vincent peering at the papers with his near-sighted eyes, I felt unsettled. I fidgeted, wondering whether we were losing valuable time. Taking tests in the manual was an entirely new experience to me. At Perkins my tests had been written in Braille, and I could go back over the questions and my answers, scanning them at will.

Suddenly Vincent transmitted the sobering news. "This is presented like an I.Q. battery test. There are at least one hundred questions here. All kinds—multiple choice, matching columns, true and false. We had better hurry."

We plunged into it without further comment. Vincent read the questions at feverish speed and I wrote with hardly less diligence. In the excitement of following his rapid manual, I sometimes murmured the answers aloud before I realized what I was doing.

"Sh-sh-h!" Vincent warned. "The other students can hear you. Keep it to yourself."

Somehow we managed to finish the test before the final

bell. Vincent handed the papers to the proctor. Then we went into the cafeteria for lunch.

One of the students came over to our table and said to me through Vincent, "You almost made me fail my exam this morning."

"What do you mean?"

"Well, I was so engrossed in watching you type out the answers that I almost forgot my own test. I had to hurry like the devil to finish it before the bell rang."

To prevent any further distraction of the other students, I was moved into the faculty's conference room on the first floor for future examinations. In history and economics the tests consisted not of the true and false variety but of composition questions. And this relieved the tension. While I settled down to pound out my essay answers Vincent would answer his mail, or do whatever other office work he had brought along to pass the time.

Upon completion of the exams, Vincent, John, and I celebrated by having dinner at a good Italian restaurant and washing down our meal with wine.

In February the results of the midyears were posted on the bulletin board, and I was delighted that I had finished among the upper 10 per cent of the class, with an average of 90 per cent.

Mr. Keane called me into his office to congratulate me. "It looks as though we have a young scholar on our hands. Bob, several newspaper reporters would like to come over to interview you. Pictures will be taken of you with Dean Meyer and Johnny for the New York papers."

I was alarmed at the thought of appearing in the newspapers. "I don't want any fuss made about this, Mr. Keane. After all, I am only at the beginning of college."

"It's only natural that the papers should want to write about you, Bob. You are the first deaf-blind man to enter college, you know."

And so the story was written, the pictures were taken. Of course I was pleased.

As time passed, a number of students at St. John's became my friends. One day, a tall, good-humored fellow came over to our table during lunch. He seated himself on one of the rickety, unsteady stools beside us and introduced himself.

"This fellow is John Donahue," John interpreted; "and he would like to know if you would care to join Sigma Tau Alpha fraternity this year."

Johnny explained the lip-reading method to him, and we were soon engaged in conversation.

"Tell me what the words Sigma Tau Alpha mean?"

"They stand for the first letters of Saint Thomas Aquinas," Donahue explained. "He's our patron saint in this society. We chose him because he is one of the greatest intellectuals who ever lived."

He went on to tell us about the aims of the group: good writing, mutual interests, and good fellowship. "And you'll have to go through the hazing, too."

We were visited shortly by a committee of three members. We were told we had to wear on campus an odd outfit consisting of a derby, knickerbockers, a red bow tie, and a wing collar.

"What! All those things belong to the past." I groaned. "Where are we going to find such antiques?"

"Don't worry," assured Johnny, "I'll look around and ask my friends. We still have two weeks before hell night to prepare ourselves."

"And what's hell night?" I wanted to know.

"The final night of the hazing, when they really make you shrink."

We were told furthermore that we must both construct whipping paddles, painted bright red with the initials of the society marked on them. John's paddle was to be three feet long; mine was to be at least eighteen inches. John solved the problem by making the paddles from slabs of wood he found at home; he painted them with red paint, then traced out the lettering with strips of white adhesive tape. We had to carry these garish things around from class to class, in addition to canes. The canes, according to specification, had to be old ones. But the real difficulty was where to find the clothing we needed. Neither of us had the slightest hope that we could ever dig up such quaint garments as knickerbockers and wing collars.

From long-forgotten sources, friends were able to produce two dusty derbies and two much-abused walking sticks. John canvassed the stores unsuccessfully; no one had the prescribed bright red bows. Instead we bought several yards of wide red ribbon, which we tied under our chins as soon as we reached the school. Knickerbockers were impossible to find even in old attics, so we improvised by rolling our pants up to the knee, leaving a generous fold in each one to give the likeness of knickers. The only thing which was easily obtainable was the short crew cut the fraternity had advised—and it had to be short!

At lunch time we were constantly badgered by other members of the society. Both of us were fined for not adhering to the original costume. I was put down for twenty paddles on hell night, and John received a quota of fifty. We were also fined fifty paddles each because our crew cuts were "not short enough." When the committee asked us to sing a duet for them, and it was revealed that we could not sing in a foreign language, we were fined additional paddle strokes. John eventually had an accumulation of over two hundred strokes to look forward to on the grand occasion of retribution, while I had one hundred and seventy strokes to my account.

One of our tormentors was John Regan, who was ultimately to become a good friend of mine. John had been a veteran of World War II—a short, stocky fellow with small mustachios and a receding hairline. He loved to sit at our table and heckle us.

Hell night arrived almost before we realized it. We were told to put on bathing trunks and sneakers and to bring our red paddles and whatever else we might be assigned by the committee. John was instructed to bring twine, a can of pea-green paint, and a brush; I was to supply a dozen eggs and a bottle of catsup. Everyone—that is, all of the new pledgees—had to bring at least one or two items to be used upon themselves on the night of expiation—dead fish, wire, needles, pins, indelible ink.

We assembled in the school gymnasium at seven o'clock in the evening. The gym was chilly; the steam had gone off and no heat radiated from the cold heaters. Attired in our skimpy wardrobes, we listened to the testing of the paddles: bang! bang! We were blindfolded and herded back to the locker room to await the opening of the celebrations.

What a medley of queer odors! The older members broke eggs over our crew-cut heads, poured catsup on top of us, stuck dead fish inside our trunks! They brought in buckets of cold water and heaved them at us. We were lined up in a row while each of us was given whacks with the paddles. We crawled over the floor, each member holding the ankles of the one preceding him, so that our knees ached from the unaccustomed rubbing. We jigged two-time to the singing of:

> . . . down to meet you in a taxi, honey;
> Better be ready 'bout half past eight.
> Oh, honey, don't be late—
> We'll be there when the band starts playing.

And all of this was punctuated periodically by the sharp tap of a paddle or the unexpected splash of ice water.

"We are going to get a fish eye," John told me, shivering from the chill of water and air. "We have to swallow it whole —or else we get fifty extra paddles."

When I was told to open my mouth and swallow I recognized the "eye of the fish" to be a large California grape. I swallowed it without difficulty.

At the close of the two hours' confusion we were once more lined up—presumably to be given the accumulated number of strokes each of us had collected during the hazing period. But actually we were led to the showers. I have never witnessed such a gruesome commingling of odors. Nor have I ever felt so sticky and unwholesome. Yellow yolk, dried to the consistency of mud, trickled down our backs; catsup and some other ill-smelling stuff—possibly vinegar or mustard— made our hair as brittle as stale cake. But it was wonderful to be under the warm spray of water, to feel the cleansing agency of soap.

Up in the conference room we were told to kneel before lighted candles while the oath of good fellowship, loyalty to St. John's, and all that was associated with its teachings was administered. It was a simple but impressive little ceremony. Then we were on our way to the Park-Vanderbilt, a restaurant where we were to have our banquet and indoctrination.

The banquet was a delicious one—thick slices of roast beef

and heaps of brown potatoes. Nothing ever tasted better to me; John agreed that it was wonderful to have something to warm us after the misery of hell night.

The first fraternity party of the season was planned to be held at the home of one of the new pledgees, in Richmond Hill. A committee was delegated to buy supplies: beer, liquors, and food; and it also had the task of arranging for dance music on records. Everyone was ready and willing, except John and me—we were unable to produce feminine partners for the occasion.

About a week before the party was scheduled we brought our problem to Mr. Keane. "Why, you poor chaps!" he exclaimed. "You really are in a predicament, aren't you? Leave it to me; I'll find two really pretty girls for both of you."

Two days before the party he called us into his office.

"I've been looking around," he told me, "and I think I've found two young ladies who will satisfy your needs. They'll be here in a moment. But first, let me ask you something—how do you feel about the fraternity?"

"It seems to be a grand group, Mr. Keane. But it also presents problems. I've never been out with a girl."

He chuckled. "Well, there is always a first time. Here come your dates right now. I want you to meet Carol and Cynthia —two of our prettiest girls in the business office of the I.H.B."

The meeting was formal. I definitely was not comfortable. I had that uneasy, self-conscious feeling I had experienced so many times in meeting strangers.

John and I agreed to pick the girls up in a taxi at Carol's home. It proved to be a long drive to Richmond Hill, and during the ride I scarcely spoke. John asked me why I was so quiet.

"Observe," I answered; "this is all new to me. I feel like another Caesar on the eve of crossing the Rubicon."

The big, roomy basement of the house in Richmond Hill was crowded; folding chairs were set up in rows and couples danced around the small groups who were seated in conversation. Someone handed me a cocktail. I began to feel more relaxed.

John Regan came over to our little group and introduced us to Frances Maas, a charming girl, with a smile that displayed small even teeth. Since Frances did not know the manual alphabet, I had to read her lips. Soon we were engrossed in conversation, discussing philosophy and poetry.

The evening was a pleasant one. I danced the rhumba for a while but, finding the floor too crowded, settled down in a small group with Johnny, Frances, John Regan, and the two girls we had brought. I tried to make conversation with Carol and Cynthia but discovered they were as shy as I was. All that I could produce in my attempts to be genial was a train of monosyllabic words.

We took the girls home in a taxi, all of us sitting in uncomfortable silence. As soon as we had left them, John commented: "They were as scared as rabbits."

"Obviously. We probably looked like refined gangsters."

Over the next few months we had other parties. Being young and full of fire is undeniably one of the happiest estates of life.

During my first year at St. John's I was required to take two semesters in apologetics. My professor in these studies was Father Charles Docherty, a Vincentian priest who eventually became not only one of my closest friends but my spiritual adviser.

I had not been in his classroom for more than two weeks when I met him personally after one of his lectures. John and

I, according to our usual habit, were slipping away to the cafeteria for a short coffee break when Father Docherty called us over to his desk.

"What does he want?" I asked John, in a whisper.

"He wants to meet you."

Feeling absurdly shy, I followed John to the front of the room, not quite certain what to expect.

"Father wants to know where you live," John interpreted.

"Over on Gates Avenue, Father."

"Louder," John instructed. "You seem to have lost your voice."

"Over on Gates Avenue."

"He wants to know if you have any family."

"Certainly I have a family—four sisters and one brother and my parents."

"Where are they?"

"At home in Pittsburgh."

"Father says he never heard of Pittsburgh—and he's smiling."

"And I never heard of Brooklyn, either." I was glad to take part in repartee.

"Father says that he would like to talk to you some afternoon when you have time. He has another class coming in now. Would next Wednesday be all right?"

"Yes—I suppose so," I said diffidently.

The following Wednesday we stayed at the college for lunch, then went to the private wing where the priests lived. We waited only a matter of minutes before Father came into the little office and shook our hands.

"Father would like to try talking to you directly with the lip-reading method," John informed me.

Father Docherty sat down beside me and took my hand, placing all five fingers on his lips.

"No, Father—not like that. I only use my thumb for reading lips."

He laughed, and I noticed that he had a warm, genuine laughter that was delightfully charming.

"Is this all right, Bob?" he asked, making the necessary change of position.

"Yes, this will be fine."

That first afternoon Father Docherty and I talked together for nearly two hours about spiritual matters. As the time passed, I acquired a growing confidence in this big Saint Bernard of a priest. His kindliness and understanding promoted a sense of deep respect. Whenever I was not certain of a doctrine which was being explained in one of my religious courses I went to him for clarification. He broke down the most complex issue into the simplest fundamentals.

"Father," I once asked him, "one of the professors is lecturing about the unity of God. What does he mean when he says that God is unique?"

"He means that there is only one God; the word 'unique' means one of a kind, and only one."

"If God is all good, Father, why do we have evil in the world?"

"There is no real evil in the world. Evil is only relative, Bob. Everything was created for a final end, and everything in itself is good when properly used. A knife is good in itself. When it is used to cut bread or meat, it is serving a good and useful end; but if you used it to murder another human being, its use would be evil."

"And what about vices like gambling or drinking alcohol, Father?"

"They only become vices when you abuse them. Drinking in moderation, Bob, is not a vice; it only becomes a grave offense when a man permits liquor to become his master and forfeits his personality to its influence. The same thing is true of gambling; it becomes offensive only when you indulge in it to excess, endangering your private means or the welfare of those who depend upon you as a provider."

The most important thing Father Docherty taught me, in all the conversations we had, was to keep an open mind, to seek for truth in all things. He taught me the invaluable lesson that no single human individual is completely free from dependence on others, that everyone is a product of the plan of a Divine Creator.

"If you pray for anything and never receive it, Bob, it's because God knows that what you desire would not help you. He is much wiser than we are—we should never question His authority, because we are finite things living in a world that is only as large as our knowledge of it."

Many an hour as we sat in Father Docherty's study, we discussed Saint Vincent de Paul, patron saint of the Vincentians to whose order Father Docherty belonged and under whose jurisdiction St. John's University is administered. Certainly Saint Vincent was an illustrious example of the Godlike spirit Father Docherty called attention to. We discussed how the seventeenth-century French saint laid the basis for organized charity in Europe, how the Sisters, enrolled in his order, entered the wards of the Hôtel-Dieu, a hospital so overcrowded that the patients were crammed sometimes six in a bed. Since many of the sufferers were victims of the plague, the doctors usually approached them saturated with disinfectants, wearing leather overcoats with goggles over their eyes and a sponge over their noses. But Vincent's Sisters simply put aprons on over their dresses and nursed them as if there were no danger of contagion.

"A man like Saint Vincent certainly presupposes the existence of a unique and benevolent God, Bob; Who else can create saints? Saint Vincent continually counseled that the only true antidote to skepticism and disbelief was a dynamic deed of love. He was fond of quoting from the Epistle of St. John: 'He that loveth not his brother whom he hath seen, how can he love God whom he hath not seen?' And to his Sisters of Charity he commanded, 'Your nunneries are the houses of the sick . . . your cloister, the streets of the city; your grille, the fear of God; your veil, holy modesty.' "

Practically to his final hour Vincent continued to live as well as teach Christianity. At seventy he charged across the Seine on horseback over a bridge flooded by rising waters. He was ravaged by recurring fevers, his kidneys became diseased, and his legs were badly swollen with rheumatism. Thrown headlong from a carriage in a collision, his life despaired of, he rallied from bed and continued on his errands of mercy until God called him home at the age of eighty-four.

"Remember, Bob, suffering for true Christians is the wine of life. It is the ability to laugh at pain that is the true measure of a man's sense of humor. And, my boy," he added gently, with a sudden squeeze of my hand, "I am certain that if there's one thing you yourself do not lack, it's a sense of humor."

The spring of my junior year my own faith and emotional maturity were put to an exacting test. Spring had come earlier than usual. Since the middle of April the weather had been extraordinarily balmy, mellow with warm sunlight and the bracing tenor of occasional breezes. As John and I passed the small park on our way to the college, there was the elusive green smell of budding leaves and young grass. But there was nothing to distinguish this particular Tuesday morning from other mornings when we walked to the old familiar building at the corner of Lewis and Willoughby.

As usual, John and I had our morning coffee in the college

cafeteria. We compared our notes, talked about the new season in baseball, then picked up our books and notes and headed for our first class in Far Eastern history. Our schedule was finished at noon, after our last period in scholastic theodicy. When the noon bell rang we hurried through the crowded halls and out to the street, walking at a brisk pace towards the Home on Gates Avenue.

After a hasty lunch in the Home's dining room I went up to my room to change clothes, slipping into a gray work uniform and a pair of old shoes. I was in the habit of working in the shop in my spare time to keep my manual skills. By one o'clock I was sitting at my machine, weaving mats. While I worked almost automatically, I reviewed the lectures of the recent classes, comparing ideas I had gained during the course of the morning.

I don't remember how long I had been working—perhaps an hour. Lou Bettica, the director of the deaf-blind department, came to me, cut the motor of my machine. "You'll have to stop for today—you're going home to Pittsburgh."

I was puzzled. "But why? Has anything happened at home?"

"Mr. Keane will tell you all about it as soon as you are finished. Come right up to the office when you're ready."

I finished the job I had been doing, closed my machine, and tidied up the table. Then I went to my room and changed again. In the office Mr. Keane was waiting for me.

"Bob, your mother is seriously ill—we aren't quite sure how seriously. You and John will take an evening plane to Pittsburgh, so pack whatever you need to take along. We have already made the necessary arrangements."

It is difficult to describe my feelings while John and I were packing my suitcase. Somehow I knew that this was more serious than I had been told; I had a peculiar sensation in my stomach, as if I had not eaten for a long time, and my muscles felt rigid. I kept saying to myself: "Mother is dying—Mother is dying."

In a sense Mr. Keane's news was not a sudden shock to me. The family had been worried for years about Mother's poor health. During my term as a senior at Perkins institute, Mother had suffered a paralytic stroke. She had been rushed to the hospital, but the doctors, unable to locate the exact position of the embolism and fearing that gangrene would set in, had been forced to amputate her leg above the knee. Her condition had been aggravated by high blood pressure and a defective heart that had been strained by overwork and worry.

It had been a harrowing experience for all of us to find Mother so suddenly bedridden. She had led such a physically active life. Belonging to the old school of housewives who believe that cleanliness is next to holiness, Mother kept her home sparkling. All of us children—including myself, to whom dust was merely a fine powder blown by the winds—were scrubbed until we were as immaculate as our surroundings. In spring and summer Mother spent her evenings working in her garden. Between the garden and the housework, there were few opportunities for rest.

I have always associated Mother in my memories with flowers. The lawn behind our house was bordered with them: roses, cockscomb, giant dahlias, tiny Japanese lanterns. Bridal bushes and honeysuckle grew along the side, and Mother increased their profusion by planting shoots and slips everywhere. On the short hill that drops away into the garden Mother made a rock garden studded with beds of low-growing, glossy plants. One of these, the lily of the valley, became my favorite when I was a child. Its cool, fresh scent, so indefinably sweet and elusive, exhilarated me. I would spend long periods of time sprawled face downward on the ground, my nose buried deep in the tiny bells which grew in crisp clusters over a big rough stone.

At first, after I lost my sight, the flowers were nameless to me, but gradually, by following my mother about while she was weeding or spading, I learned to know them by their shapes, and characteristic growth. Some of the blossoms had such an irresistible scent that I would pluck petals to nibble on them, only to find that they were bitter or sour to the taste. But there were the petunias that grew in a great red clay pot in the center of the back lawn. I soon discovered that early in the morning, before the sun had dried them out, the fragrant corollas had a drop of nectar at their bases which was as sweet as honeydew. To my mother's chagrin, I plucked nearly all the blossoms as soon as they came into bloom.

When a rosebush died or a flower was broken Mother was sad. She loved these growing things—their beauty, their symmetry, their colored glory and fragrance. On our window sill in the big kitchen slips of green plants sprouted in slender wineglasses of water, and there were pots of tangy geraniums and wax begonias. Perhaps the Chinese proverb is true when it says, "In the faces of flowers the heart of God is revealed."

And now, like a bolt out of the blue, Mother had been crippled by a stroke, cut off from the things she loved. We, in our consternation, failed to measure her true gallantry of spirit. She who had partaken of life so zestfully resisted being deprived of its essential consolations. Within a matter of weeks after her operation she demanded a wheel chair and had her bedroom moved downstairs to the living room, where she could be near the kitchen. Before long she was wheeling her chair about, cooking meals, dusting as she had always done. She would stand up, clutching anything that offered support, and in spite of my father's vehement protests she insisted in continuing where she had left off.

Yet we all realized she was seriously ill. There were days when she could not rise from bed, and she became irritable as a child.

She was fitted for an artificial leg, but she was never able to use it without carrying crutches, and she could only use it when there were fleeting periods of unusual health. But whenever visitors came to the house she would insist on putting it on. Genuinely feminine, she had that endearing vanity to "look her best" for company.

All the memories I had of Mother's suffering over the last four years passed through my mind now as Johnny and I drove out to La Guardia to make the evening plane. This was my first trip by air, yet I could not concentrate on what was happening. I hoped, I prayed, that I would reach my home before it was too late. I had often prayed before, but never with such a sense of futility.

I must have fallen asleep, for the next thing I knew was that my ears were ringing and suddenly painful. The pressure of the cabin was unbearable. I asked John how much longer we would be in the air.

"Fifteen minutes."

When the plane landed we took a taxi to my home. Olga, my sister, met us at the door—a quiet, uncertain Olga who threw her arms around my neck and hugged me so tightly that I thought she would never let go. Finally she released me. "Mom has had another stroke, Bob. The doctor says she won't live for more than a day or two. We don't know whether she can hear or see; she just lies there quietly." Olga began to cry—softly, uncontrollably. She took my hand.

The rest of the family were waiting for me in the upper hall—Lillian, Ruth, my brother Bill, and my father. All of them were subdued; my father barely greeted me, so deeply moved that he had temporarily lost interest in what was taking place about him. Ruth, my youngest sister and a professional nurse, appeared to be in charge. She had taken leave of her hospital duties in order to be with my mother.

Though Ruth had a reputation for being calmly efficient in her duties as a surgical nurse, when one of the family became ill she lost her positiveness. Now she was quiet like the others, and I noticed a tremor in her voice. "Do you want to come in and see Mother now?"

I nodded. She led me into the bedroom and I walked up to the side of the bed, moving my hand along until it found the pillow. I touched my mother's shoulder, ran my fingers lightly down her arm until I was holding her hand.

"Mom! This is Bob. Don't you know me?"

The fingers I was holding began to move, to tremble, as if some feeling of recognition had passed into them. I remembered what Olga had said, that it was doubtful whether Mother could see or hear, yet I felt certain that she knew me. She had held my hand so many times before.

I released her hand gently and moved my own up toward her face. It was hot with fever and suffering. But I was totally unprepared for the terrible sound I felt beneath my finger tips—the rasping, gurgling sound of the death rattle. I stood there, immovably transfixed, realizing that she was slowly choking. Then I turned away, sick at heart, leaving the room as swiftly as I could. My own throat was horribly constricted with dry sobs which I did not want to show—I had not cried for many years.

John came to me at the door, but I pushed him away, unable to express myself in words. I went into another room and closed the door; I sat down on a chair and waited until I had my control again. For the rest of the night I did not return to the sickroom, fearing that I would once again have the same feeling of pity and sadness and futility.

Through the small hours before dawn we all sat in the next room, drinking endless cups of coffee. We talked about Mother—how she loved beautiful things, how she had reared us and watched over us. They kept saying, "She knew you, Bob; she recognized you—it was the first time we've seen her move for days." They told me to go down and stretch out on the sofa to sleep, but I refused. Ruth put a sleeping draught into my coffee, but I fought off the desire to sleep.

At six o'clock Ruth came into the room. She was crying softly. We understood. We followed her into the sickroom, stunned. "Look, Bob," Ruth said to me, "Mother is smiling. Look—she's smiling!" Slowly I passed my fingers over that calm, imperturbable face, knowing that this was the last smile my mother would ever share with us—and then I hurried out.

Father had fallen asleep on his bed, completely exhausted by the strain of watching. I woke him and said, "Mom is gone, Dad." He did not answer; he rose quickly and hurried away, a little more stooped than I had ever seen him.

I slipped into an empty room and found a comfortable chair. Mother had received the last sacrament; I could imagine the robed priest bestowing his final blessing on her forehead. A stray phrase of Latin came to my mind: "*Te absolvo in nomine Patris, et Filii, et Spiritus Sanctus.*" Mother had loved those rituals, with all their ceremony and sonorous pronouncements. I began to be drowsy; the drug Ruth had given me was taking effect. My mind was full of broken phrases of Scripture. "And behold, there was a great earthquake; for an angel of the Lord came down from heaven, and drawing near rolled away the stone, and sat upon it. His countenance was like lightning and his raiment like snow." Surely the gates had been opened to her, too— she who had been so gallant of spirit, so pure of heart. As I drifted toward sleep, I wondered if she had been saying to herself, "I will go unto God, unto God Who is the joy of my youth." It would have been so like her.

I awoke a few hours later, feeling the same weight of depression I had known during the night. After breakfast John and I walked along the streets for a while. I knew that he was uncomfortable with us, so I suggested that he take a plane back to New York. He left in the early afternoon.

Mother's coffin was at home—she had insisted upon it, saying that funeral parlors were undignified. Visitors and relatives and friends swarmed to the house, bringing flowers. The funeral director said that he had never seen so many flowers; the rooms were piled high with them, all available space being covered with lilies and roses and other blooms. The air was insufferably permeated with the mingled fragrances.

I wandered about aimlessly, uncertain whether I should be present or go somewhere out of the way. When night came we recited the Rosary, all of us kneeling in a semicircle in front of the casket. Then everyone was gone—except Lillian, Olga, and myself, who chose to stay awake and watch.

For the next two nights I was sleepless. Sometimes I would wander into the room where the casket lay, kneel down beside it and search until I felt my mother's hands. They were cold, with a curious waxen resilience, folded over her bosom and clutching her rosary. I would pretend that she was asleep, not really gone forever.

> The house is full of her. In every room
> I sense her presence moving everywhere—
> A quiet radiance, and a dim perfume,
> That haunt the darkest corner of the stair.

Life at My Fingertips

This is the vase her fingers once caressed
So fondly as she filled its heart with flowers;
Here is the missal that her warm lips pressed
In times of joy or melancholy hours.

She is not here; and yet she seems to be
A living part of these familiar things,
As if her soul had spanned Eternity
To hover close to me on viewless wings;
Guarding me still, and smiling as I touch
These souvenirs she once had loved so much.

On the morning of the funeral, shortly before the closing of the casket, I was surprised to discover that Father Docherty had arrived. He met me at the door, his face unsmiling but his voice full of warmth and sympathy. "I thought I would drop in and see you, Bob. How is everything?"

"All right, Father. Will you come with me and see her before they close the coffin?"

We went into the room and knelt beside it. Father Docherty said a short prayer. As we rose to go, he turned to me. "Remember, Bob, how much she loved you and now she is with God. Be happy that you could keep her for such a long time, and thank Him for the privilege of having known her."

The funeral cortege wound its way down the long hill to the Church of St. Norbert's. Father Docherty assisted the parish priest at Mass, and I have always considered his kindness one of the greatest favors I have received. I sat between my father and my sister Olga. When we knelt together, near the end of the service, I knew that the coffin was being closed. I felt my father's shoulder against mine, trembling spasmodically; and on the other side Olga gripped my hand, her tears falling on my fingers and rolling away. Then it was over and we were in a car moving toward the cemetery.

"I Sense Her Presence Everywhere"

The funeral procession through the cemetery was a slow, painful one. The day was still, sunless, and with a heavy overcast sky. There was that peculiar heaviness of air that made me think that even the angels were mourning. The smell of new-turned earth struck my nostrils and made me unhappily aware of the final moment.

We stood a little while on the soft earth at the brink of the grave. Someone gave me a handful of flower petals; I threw them down into the opening. There was a short prayer, and we turned away. My father dragged his feet, his head was bent, and he was sobbing convulsively. He had been married for nearly forty years to Mother; it was difficult for him to leave her now. I threw my arm about his shoulders to support him, and Joe, my sister Olga's husband, came to take his other arm. Between us, we led him back to the car—his eyes blinded with tears, his feet stumbling over the broken earth.

And then I felt the presence of Father Docherty, walking quietly at my side. And all at once I recalled words he had once spoken: "In a garden, Bob, where a single lovely shape is reproduced not once but countless thousands of times, year after year, one becomes aware that there is a Lawgiver, Who is the soul of the Universe. Only the skeptic can look upon these perfect symbols and declare that the world he lives in is nothing but a chance happening without an explanation."

Chapter V

Betty

My world is a curious one, set apart from the rush of human affairs. To others it is as impenetrable as the waters of the sea. But to me it is the home where I live busily with memories, hopes, pleasures. Among the shadows are the beautiful pictures of the past—each as vivid as a bright star in a black sky. Familiar forms and faces are there, faces that have come a long way from the past and others that are distinct and enhanced by imagination. They never stand still, but turn and change, shifting through well-remembered scenes.

One mellowing, sobering experience took place during the summer before my junior year at St. John's University.

The Industrial Home, with an eye to my postgraduate career, had decided to send me to the University of Michigan's School of Special Education, to take courses in the vocational rehabilitation of the blind.

When Mr. Keane called Johnny and me into his office and announced that we were to attend six weeks of summer schooling, we were depressed, for we had hoped to idle away the summer.

However, we prepared ourselves for the new regimen. One evening in June we packed our luggage and a Braille writer into a taxi and hurried off to Grand Central Station.

On board the train, unable to sleep, we sat in our small, cramped bedroom. John suggested we order some beer; he rang for the porter. We struck up a conversation about the prospects of the current baseball season; and we exchanged remarks about the blissfulness of vacations. "I'd have loved to have gone up to Canada," John confided wistfully.

"And I'd just as soon be home with my family and a few good novels to read."

The porter woke us early next morning. We dressed, ate breakfast in the dining car, and were ready for the change of trains when we reached Detroit. A little after nine o'clock we stepped onto the platform in Ypsilanti, Michigan. We called a taxi and drove over to the college.

"Real rural campus," John commented. "Lots of buildings, trees and grounds. Maybe it won't be so dull."

We were assigned rooms in Munson Hall as soon as we checked in with the office. We were registered for three courses—psychology, history of blindness, and social work; and then we headed for our quarters. Our rooms consisted of a small study and bedroom, which we were to share together.

Within the first couple of days we settled down to the routine of college work, attending classes, studying our notes and reading the textbooks we found in the library. But we found it rather dreary. In the evenings we took walks through the campus and the town of Ypsilanti. Then one Thursday evening during the second week, John announced: "I was talking to Bill Scanlon in the shower room. He says they're having a dance tonight at the Center; would you like to go along?"

"Not me." I had not as yet gotten completely over my shyness at meeting strangers. "I'd be absolutely out of place. You can go there, though. I'll stay here and finish some of my studying."

"Oh, come on. The change will be good for you. Why live like a hermit?"

Finally I agreed to accompany him. At eight o'clock in the evening I selected a pipe, filled my pouch full of tobacco, and headed with John for the Center. John found me a comfortable chair along the side of the room where the couples were moving about in a quick foxtrot. I leaned back, lit my pipe, and tried to follow the rhythm of the music as it vibrated in the air. I had been sitting there for more than half an hour when John came back.

"Wouldn't you like to dance? There's a nice girl here—a coed taking courses in occupational therapy at the university. She would like to meet you."

"Sorry, old chap. Please thank her for the thought; I'll just sit here and meditate upon my virtues."

"She wants to talk to you," John persisted. "Don't be so dastardly. Talk to her, just for a few minutes."

"What's her name?"

"Betty. She doesn't know the manual alphabet, so you'll have to read her lips."

"Suppose I can't read them?"

"Don't be so stubborn."

Betty sat down beside me and took my hand. "How are you, Bob?" she asked in a pleasant, rather husky voice.

Betty and I became close friends. Acting as a volunteer to help some of our blind students, she took her meals in the dining room that had been assigned especially to our group. She came over to my table to talk to me after meals. I don't remember how it happened, but soon I began calling her "Mama Betty," a pet name which made her smile.

"What's new, Mama Betty?"

"Sh-sh-sh," she'd say. "Don't call me that any more. The others are already starting to call me it too."

"Do you mind? After all, it's only a joke."

"I don't really mind, but before you know it, they'll start calling you papa."

"Papa Bob," I muttered. "It sounds sort of like a motorboat—all those puffing sounds."

Not being less curious than the next person, I had asked John at the outset whether Betty had made a favorable impression on him. "What does she look like?"

"So you're interested? Well, she's athletic-looking; she has that sort of brown hair you call chestnut; blue eyes, I think, and a pleasant face. She has lots of personality."

"I know about the personality. All I wondered about was whether she was reasonably nice to look at."

Betty and I went to nearly all of the dances together, yet it was always arranged that we were part of a group. Gradually I began to wonder whether she would accept if I invited her alone to a dinner in town. Halfway through the summer I got up the courage to ask her.

"Would you like to go to the Hotel Huron for dinner with me, Bet—just the two of us?"

"I'd love to go, Bob. I thought you were never going to invite me."

"How shall we plan it?"

"I'll pick you up in the lobby of Munson Hall, Bob, around six o'clock. We'll be at the hotel in about ten minutes."

Betty

When we arrived at the hotel we found a table in a corner of the dining room where we could sit and catch a faint breeze from a window. We ordered sherry and broiled steaks. The drink temporarily calmed my nervousness so that I could talk with reasonable freedom. But when the food arrived I found that my hand was shaking from excitement. I could barely hold the silver steady while I cut my steak.

"Let me do that for you." Betty took the knife away. "You'll be cutting up your necktie soon."

I relinquished the silverware gratefully. "Will you join me in another glass of sherry?"

"That's enough for you, Bob. Just relax and enjoy your dinner."

I doubt whether I have ever eaten a dinner with more fastidious care. When coffee and dessert were served I felt more comfortable. I positively sparkled with anecdotes and small talk.

After dinner we walked back along Lake Michigan and returned to Goodison Hall where Betty lived. We went into a paneled study leading off from the sitting room. Betty sat down at a piano and played it, to entertain me. I stood beside her, my hand resting on the vibrating surface of the instrument, detecting chords interspersed with rippling notes that rose and fell sharply in crescendos.

"Come, Betty. Play me a Viennese waltz. Waltz time is admirably compatible with me. I must have a metronome in my soul."

I followed the rhythm of her melody, tapping with my foot on the thick pile of the carpet. When it was finished Betty paused again, and then her fingers rippled over the keys. The melody she was playing seemed oddly familiar, so I gave it my full attention.

"You are playing the Moonlight Sonata, Betty."

She dropped her hands from the keys and turned around on the bench. I could feel her looking up at me. "You can recognize it?"

"One of my schoolmates used to play it quite often while I was at Perkins. But I wasn't quite sure—it's been so long since I heard it last."

I was speaking figuratively when I said "heard it." Of course, I meant "felt it." After all, the sense of hearing is merely the vibration of the tympanums in the ear. Even though one could scarcely say that fingertips are as sensitive, they nevertheless pick up quite a lot of vibration— like lip reading, or feeling the music of a song.

During the following weeks Betty and I went out alone frequently. Betty learned the manual alphabet from me in a surprisingly short time; it only required half an hour to teach her the various positions of the fingers in forming the letters. It was while we were taking a fellow student to the airport one hot July afternoon that she had asked me to teach her.

"Why do you want to learn it, Betty? We seem to communicate admirably through lip reading. If you learn the alphabet, I won't be able to watch you smile."

"But I can't say everything I'd like to say—especially when other people are listening to us. I want to tell you secrets."

"Very well, then, let's begin."

I was delighted with her progress. Even before we arrived back at the campus Betty was spelling out sentences. Turning to John, who was sitting in the rear of the car, I teased: "What do you think of this; Betty has surpassed you. If I remember correctly, I had a dudgeon of a time trying to teach you the alphabet."

"Don't make comparisons. She's had you for inspiration."

"You had me for inspiration, too—and look how long it took you to become proficient."

"It's not the same idea, old boy. I didn't fall in love with you at first sight."

"Oh, don't be facetious!" My face grew suddenly uncomfortably warm.

Betty squeezed my hand. "Don't listen to him," she laughed. "He's only needling us."

I continued to feel a growing affection for this warmhearted, good-humored girl from Ohio, but I never fully appreciated how strongly attracted I was to her until the night we went to a lakeside night club. It was a Saturday evening, with a hint of falling dew pervading the country night. Eight of us students somehow crammed ourselves into one car and drove out along the highway to the lake.

When we arrived two tables were pushed together for us. We called the waiter and ordered drinks.

"Why are you so quiet tonight?" Betty was sensitive to my brooding.

"I don't think I can fool you, Bet. I'm a trifle self-conscious."

"Oh, forget it all. Let's dance."

We moved out onto the dance floor. It was pleasant to float along to the slow rhythm of the music, and I could feel Betty humming the tune as we moved among the other dancing couples. As her hair brushed against my cheek I caught the faint, delicate odor of perfume. I held her a little closer.

"Are you enjoying yourself, Bob?"

"You know I enjoy being with you anywhere."

"I'm having a wonderful time too."

The evening ended much too soon. At eleven-thirty we picked up our coats and hurried out to the car. Curfew was set for twelve-thirty at Goodison Hall.

In the car I leaned back in my seat. "It's been a wonderful evening."

"Grand. I never enjoyed anything so much. I didn't know you could dance so well."

"Neither did I. You must have inspired me."

I held her closer. "May I kiss you?"

"Of course—don't be ridiculous. You never ask girls such questions."

Her lips were soft and warm, and I had an odd sensation of being very close to her.

We kissed again; then I sat quietly, content to feel her head resting against my shoulder, her soft hair whispering against my cheek in the rush of the night air as the car moved onward.

We dropped the girls at Goodison, then drove leisurely back to Munson Hall.

Once in bed, it took me a long time to drift off to sleep. I kept tossing about restlessly, not being able to stay in any one position long enough to relax. Most discouraging, I thought to myself; you meet a lovely girl and then you can't forget her. I had a deep conviction that I was falling in love with Betty. When I finally fell asleep I dreamed of being in a car with her, moving swiftly through the night.

Betty and I saw each other every day during the following weeks; we met in the common dining room where we took our meals, and in the evenings we were always together. Sometimes we joined groups of students and went to a rendezvous in town, but more often we strolled about the campus, or down by the lake. It was pleasant to find a seat on one of the benches in a quiet spot; we would sit there for hours in the evening air, talking about whatever interested us at the moment.

I learned that Betty was the daughter of a country lawyer from a small town in Ohio. Her father, she told me, had plenty of competition from other lawyers in the town. Her younger brothers were in college, one preparing for the law, another in a seminary preparing for the priesthood. Betty was studying occupational therapy, and she was in her senior year at the university.

We talked about everything under the stars; Betty's plans for becoming an occupational therapist, and what I might do when I finished my studies at St. John's. It was pleasant to sit there, our feet ankle-deep in tall grass, and the scent of water and green things coming up to us from the lake bank. Betty asked:

"Have you ever thought of getting married someday, Bob?"

"What is this?" I quipped. "A proposal?"

"Of course not. But everyone thinks about things like that."

"Rather a sudden question, isn't it? Seriously, though, I've never thought of it before—at least, never with any real interest. But I like you, Betty."

"I like you, too, Bob."

We sat close together. After a bit, Betty persisted with her question. "Bob, why have you not thought seriously about marriage?"

"I still have to finish college, Betty. And when I graduate the future seems so uncertain."

"But would you marry once you become settled?"

"I don't know, Bet. I've been brought up with an old-fashioned philosophy. I'd feel under an obligation to give my girl all the happiness I could, and I'm not sure whether I'd be equal to it. I hate being dependent on anyone. I'm not afraid of responsibilities, but when I think of the problems involved, how much I would need to rely on the girl I might marry, I feel like a heel. The important thing is that she should be happy."

"But suppose the girl really loves you, Bob, and wants to help you because of yourself?"

"It's too much of a sacrifice."

"That's nonsense. You're intelligent enough to realize that no woman would marry you unless she really loved you. Nothing else matters."

She was so serious that I bent over and kissed her. She put her arms around my neck and held me tightly.

"I must be dreaming, Bet."

"So am I." She paused. "Bob, the summer is almost over. We'll soon be saying good-by. . . . Are you going to invite me to your college dances?"

"I'd love to, but perhaps you'll change your mind, after we say good-by."

"I won't change."

A light breeze came up out of nowhere and blew a wisp of her hair against my cheek; I could smell a faint perfume from its softness. Neither of us wanted to leave.

When our six-week session of study at the university ended, the business of saying good-by to Betty was a painful one. I had become genuinely fond of this girl with the spontaneous good-humored laughter, and the charming, candid personality. I kept wondering how I would express my feelings toward her at the last minute.

On the last day, half an hour before John and I were to

leave for the afternoon plane, Betty came over to Munson Hall to say good-by. We stood in a corner of the deserted lobby and talked trivialities. John had discreetly slipped away to check on final arrangements.

"Only five minutes to go." I glanced at my wrist watch. "Time flies too fast for me."

"I'm going to miss you, Bob—I've had such a wonderful time."

"So have I—and I hate to say good-by. Good-bys always seem to have such finality. Please write to me sometimes when you're not too busy with your studies or the other fellows."

"There won't be any other fellows—don't say it. And remember, you've promised to invite me to a prom."

I kissed her and held her for a long while. Neither of us said anything—there was nothing more to say, and we both understood.

"John is coming back now," Betty told me, drawing away. "Please don't forget me."

"How could I forget?"

John came up to us and dropped the suitcases he was carrying. "It's time to leave. The taxi is right out in front."

I kissed Betty and picked up one of the bags. We moved out of the door into the sunlight. As the taxi gathered speed and headed toward the station on the other side of town, I sat back and tried to appraise the future. It was useless. I could only think of Betty and wonder whether we would ever see each other again. . . .

Rich and beautiful is my love, my dearest—
As soft and pure as snow that falls on snow;
Sweet as mulled wine that holds the candle's glow,
That warms the blood and sparkles in the eyes.

And the great white stars shall dim with age, my dearest,
And all earth's winds shall sigh themselves to sleep;
Then, like a whispered prayer, my love shall leap
Straight through the gilded gates of Paradise.

During the next few weeks after my return to Brooklyn I found myself thinking constantly about Betty. I would find myself daydreaming at odd moments when I was unoccupied; my mind would return to those summer evenings along Lake Huron, or to some nook of the college campus where we had been accustomed to sit and talk away the hours. At times like these I would wish that the summer had gone on forever.

John noticed my spells of silence and commented on them. "What are you dreaming about now?"

"Not a blessed thing," I'd answer evasively.

The letters Betty wrote me mirrored her personality perfectly. They always ended: "God bless you, Bob; and please remember me in your prayers."

Invariably they stirred my memory of insignificant little conversations we had shared. Like the evening under the maple with the trysting bench around it, when I had asked, rather hesitantly, whether she had ever been in love before.

"Of course, it isn't any of my business, but I am rather curious. I was born with curiosity flowing in my veins."

"I don't see why I shouldn't answer that question, Bob. There was someone, but I don't think I was ever really interested in him—not genuinely."

"Why not?"

"He used to ask me how many children I wanted."

"What was your answer?"

"I told him to mind his own business."

"Don't you like children?"

"Of course I do—I love them. When I'm at home I always have a bunch of the neighbors' children with me, and we have a grand time."

"I don't quite comprehend it. What do you really expect in life—in marriage, for instance?"

"I want to marry someone who needs me—someone I can help. I want to be useful to him."

She said this with such simplicity that it was impossible for me to doubt her sincerity.

As the weeks lengthened into months, I began to assume that the affair had been nothing more than a passing episode. Gradually our correspondence had fallen off, so that I believed Betty was preoccupied with her postgraduate studies, or perhaps turning her affections to someone else.

In the meantime I continued to pursue my studies, which had become increasingly complex. On the night of my twenty-fourth birthday the deaf-blind men of the I.H.B. gave me a party at the clubhouse in Brooklyn. It was a gay party, and all my friends were there. About nine o'clock Johnny said to me: "We have a little surprise for you. We'll have to leave right now in order to get to the airport on time."

"Who's coming in on the plane?"

"Wait and see."

We took a taxi to La Guardia, speeding through the heavy traffic at the breakneck pace all New Yorkers use. When we arrived we hurried over to a window and John had the incoming flights checked.

"Look who's coming!" John said suddenly. Before I realized it, Betty was standing beside me, kissing me on the cheek.

"It's wonderful to see you, Bob." She stepped back a little to look at me.

I was stunned. "Who could have believed it?" I murmured. "Who could have believed it?"

John hustled us into a taxi, and we drove to the Towers Hotel in Brooklyn. We spent the evening talking about the old days in Michigan. I realized Betty hadn't changed at all; she was the same girl I had known—witty, practical, and devoted. My old desire to be near her, which had lain dormant for so long, sprang into life again.

The lounge where we were sitting closed shortly after one o'clock, so John and I escorted Betty to the elevator and to her room. The evening had seemed incredibly short-lived.

We stopped at Betty's door. "It's been so wonderful, seeing you again." I kissed her good night. "I thought you might have changed, but you haven't."

"I told you I wouldn't. And I've missed you all this time."

Next morning I introduced Betty to Mr. Keane. Later he said to me aside, "Betty is the kind of girl I would have picked for you myself, Bob."

"Hold on, Mr. Keane; I'm not ready for the altar yet."

The three of us—John, Betty, and I—went into Manhattan for dinner that evening. And after dinner we walked through the streets for a while. Betty wanted to ride in the subway, but John advised us that we wouldn't have time; we were to meet friends at the hotel for a small party. We decided to take a taxi back to Brooklyn.

"Why are you so quiet?" Betty put her head on my shoulder.

"I didn't know I was being quiet."

"What are you thinking about?"

"Nothing in particular. What makes you so certain that I am thinking?"

"You seem so thoughtful. Do you still love me?"

"Should I answer that question now?" I answered evasively. "You forget that John is with us."

"Tell me later, then."

But there never was a chance to be alone together; I made certain that someone would always be with us, for I was gripped with a tremendous sense of inadequacy. The idea of marriage had become so real that I found myself unable to face it. I kept repeating to myself Francis William Bourdillon's thought that "the mind has a thousand eyes, and the heart but one." I realized that I was faced by an important decision which, if I arrived at it affirmatively, could bring about happiness. But at the same time I knew that it would also mean hazarding a blind guess into the future. If I continued my relationship with Betty, it would ultimately lead to marriage, and marriage would necessarily entail problems of security. My heart told me that Betty would be willing to undertake any hardships that might occur; but my mind reasoned that I ought not to perpetrate undue obligations upon her devotedness. At the moment I was absolutely at a low ebb in finances, and I had not the slightest idea what my prospects would be within the next few years. I wanted Betty to be happy, to have everything that would give her comfort. I felt that it was my strongest responsibility to prove that I could provide at least the fundamentals which any intelligent, high-spirited girl would naturally expect. And, to crown the whole situation, I became acutely self-conscious of my disabilities—disabilities that now asserted themselves with fresh and overwhelming urgency.

I thought I would manage the breach with Betty with tactful diplomacy, but I soon abandoned the idea, knowing that Betty—with her penetrating insight—would recognize my phrases for what they actually were, nothing but lame excuses. "You're making a terrible blunder," my impulsive nature told me; "Betty would be willing to go through anything if you merely asked." But my reason—or was it conscience in another form?—insisted that I had no right to subject anyone to such self-denial.

The only logical way out seemed to be to break off our relationship abruptly, without trying to justify myself by explanations. When Betty went back to Michigan I decided not to write to her again, although the decision was the hardest I had ever faced. One afternoon Mr. Keane brought up the subject of marriage, and I felt extremely uncomfortable.

"Have you ever thought of being married, my lad?"

"Of course."

"How about Betty, then?"

"I'm sorry to disappoint you, Mr. Keane, but I've broken off the little romance we had."

"Good Lord—what for? She is a grand girl. She has everything you could wish for."

"I know that. But I felt too inadequate. How could I support her when I'm just beginning?"

"There's always a little struggle at first, you know."

"Yes, I know that. I think you realize, though, that my disabilities would make it more difficult for us to begin a real life than it might be for other people."

Betty wrote to me several times during the summer; and when I failed to respond she wrote to Father Docherty to ask him why I never answered her letters. The priest was concerned; he had met Betty and taken a liking to her, and, being a close friend of mine, he was always eager to be of assistance. On one of his visits he broached the subject with his usual tact.

"I have something to say to you, Bob; I'm not trying to be intrusive; I only want to help you. Betty has written a letter to me, and she feels quite hurt that you never write to her any more. She really regards you with affection and she thinks you respond. My problem is what to write to her? You'll have to give me some kind of explanation to pass on to her."

I thought for a moment. "This is a difficult situation for me, Father. I know that Betty is fond of me, and the last thing I want to do is hurt her feelings. I have two serious drawbacks in my deafness and blindness. One disability would not have been so serious; two are too many. I can see a host of problems that would arise—and I know you realize most of them. If I wrote to Betty now and explained everything, it would still be painful for both of us. I feel that it's much easier for me to simply drop the whole situation without any further action. I hope that Betty will find someone else who is more suitable than I am. As time goes by, I think both of us will forget about the whole thing."

For a long time afterward in unguarded moments I felt an overpowering sense of guilt. I wondered once again, as I had wondered many times before, whether my decision to remain silent, to avoid future contacts with Betty was not a brutal and ungallant action. Love can be such a terrible dilemma, especially when one's heart dictates a course of impulsiveness and the mind holds forth with rationalizations. To fall in love is a painful experience, for long after the wounds have healed there is always the memory of having known a precious thing and lost it in the confusion of one's own misgivings.

It was two years before I summoned up the courage to write to Betty again. One day, in a spirit of curiosity, I addressed a letter to her at her home in Ohio. A week later

I received a reply—a letter which told about her marriage and the birth of her first son. I was delighted. Life, I thought, has a great many twistings and turnings, yet there was always the possibility of finding a rainbow of contentment after the storm.

I felt happy for Betty; she deserved so much from life. And I feel deeply that there will be another Betty someday for me, that I will find happiness in building a family, and I look forward eagerly to the challenges it will bring.

Chapter VI

Graduation

I HAVE often tried to evaluate the influences in my life; and yet I have never been satisfied with the conclusions I have reached. People and places and atmospheres—all of these have been incorporated into my personality so gradually that I have not always been aware of them. Looking back over the early years of my childhood, I am continually bemused by the vision of the little boy who was governed by instinct rather than reason, who was rebellious and fractious, prone to selfish motives. Even parental love and the affections of my brothers and sisters could not sweeten my rampant nature.

Through the years I have remained close to my family. Since Mother's funeral I have been particularly anxious to visit my father to lessen his loneliness. Mother had nurtured in me an undying love for home; and her death only served to strengthen it, for her presence really never left our house.

Usually my visits are made twice a year, at Christmas and summer-vacation time. I arrive home in Pittsburgh late at night, but Father has never hesitated to rise to the occasion. As soon as he hears my sister Olga's excited voice, he comes padding down the stairs in his old slippers, his warm, capable hand outstretched in greeting. We play the little game that we have played for years now.

"Well, son, are you married yet?"

"Not that I know of, Dad. Why? Are you in a hurry to be a grandfather again?"

"I thought maybe you had a nice girl in New York. You're getting pretty old, so you'd better hurry up."

Out in the kitchen Olga sets about brewing coffee and making a light lunch. Her husband, Joe, comes down to join us, and we spend half the night discussing all that has happened in the months since I have been with them last. Even after Joe and Father have gone back to sleep, Olga and I sit late into the night, exchanging gossip.

"Well, it's almost four o'clock, and I must be up early tomorrow to do the shopping," Olga finally says, draining her coffee cup. "The children will be glad to see you in the morning—they've all been asking for you."

"I've brought them a few small gifts—water pistols for the boys and paint sets for the girls."

"Don't you dare! They'll have the house in a mess in jig time."

In the morning the children come trooping into my room. Jimmy, Olga's youngest, hurtles onto my bed with a laugh. Patty is there, too, very much a young lady for her ten years; and Joey, the eldest, with his mass of soft, curly hair. Soon—after I have gone down to breakfast—they are joined by my other sister Lil and her children: Don, with his good-natured grin; Janet, a petite young lady already growing into womanhood at sixteen; Michael, my godson; and little Ruth, a bundle of dynamic vitality who is impetuously affectionate.

It seems incredible to me that, only a few short years before, I had held each one in my arms, a bundle of wriggling infant life.

Vacation time affords me the opportunity of reading books at leisure; and when I am not reading Olga and I sit down to sessions of rummy, or the children plead for stories. "Let's play Chinese checkers, Uncle Bob."

"I'm a bit lazy today, Joey."

"Oh, come on, Uncle Bob—just one or two games."

But if I play Chinese checkers with Joey, Patty demands her share of entertainment too. She leans against my shoulder. "Tell me a story. Tell me about Rumpelstiltskin or Bluebeard."

"Go away, Patty—go away. I have forgotten all those stories."

"You're a fibber, Uncle Bob. You can't fool me."

I allow myself to be led to the living room, pushed into an armchair; Patty and Jimmy climb into my lap. And if I happen to be out on the porch, I find myself surrounded by moppets from the neighborhood.

> I'll tell you a story of Jack of Madory,
> And now my story's begun;
> I'll tell you another of Jack and his brother—
> And now my story is done.

"Uncle Bob! Please, I want to hear Bluebeard."

Bluebeard is invariably followed by the "Ghost with Three Toes," and "Hänsel and Gretel." Like most raconteurs, I enjoy myself hugely; the children sit quietly as if they were in church. It always reminds me of Longfellow's poem, *The Children's Hour*, and I fancy that the poet had experienced the same sensation of pleasure I feel.

Of all children, Patty is one of my favorites. Recently I wrote a poem for her.

For My Niece

My darling, you are still too young to know
What makes these pretty trees and flowers grow,
Who lights the bright lamps of the stars at night,
And fills the morning skies with lakes of light.

Your dreams are full of fairies, old and wise;
They throw their shining stardust in your eyes
So that you see, in every lonely place,
The smiling of a kindly, wrinkled face.

You hear their lilting laughter in the rain,
Their dancing footsteps running through the lane,
And when the day is done, you nod and sigh,
Listening for their evening lullaby.

You see and hear these things I saw and heard
When I was young, before my senses blurred;
So when I press your tiny, dimpled hand,
It is to let you know—I understand.

During the balance of my college education I continued to meet with Father Docherty at least once a week to talk about the certainty of God amidst inscrutable happenings.

Speaking of God's love, Father was fond of a saying of Pascal. "The heart has its reasons which reason knows nothing of." Father presented me one day with a medallion of the Virgin Mother to wear on a chain around my neck.

"This will take good care of you, my boy. Wear it always. Remember, if we meet no gods it is because we harbor none."

Graduation

One Sunday in the fall of my junior year I had an appointment to go with Harry Weitman, my roommate at the Home, to dinner with his brother and sister-in-law in Corona, New York.

"I think it is not so nice for us to go to dinner with George and Betty unless we give them a little something," Harry suggested in his quaint, idiomatic way. "It is better for us to give them good chocolate. It will make us feel good. Do you like my idea?"

"I'll go out and buy the chocolates. It will take only fifteen minutes."

"I think it is not so good for you to go alone," Harry said worriedly. "Better if you cross with Wilfred. He can see a little light and find the store fast. Save time—save trouble."

Harry, fifteen years my senior, had always been paternal toward me. In his fussy way he was continually enjoining me to be careful.

"All right," I told him, slipping into my jacket and picking up my cane. "I'll call Wilfred."

Wilfred, one of our deaf men with limited vision, was sitting in the smoking room, puffing away on a pipe. When I asked him to accompany me he said, "Sure! sure!" He never seemed able to refuse anyone a favor.

It was nearly two o'clock when Wilfred Couturier and I opened the door and started down the front walk. We turned to the right, heading towards Tompkins Avenue and the crosswalk. At the corner we stopped.

"Wait," I said. "Don't cross until someone comes to help us. Understand?"

"Sure, sure," Wilfred answered, but I wasn't positive he had been reading my hand properly. The chill of the December afternoon had numbed our fingers, and I knew that Wilfred was not a sensitive reader even under ordinary circumstances. I repeated my injunction and received the same reply. Nevertheless, I felt uneasy, as I always did when I went out with him.

"Red now," he said suddenly, pointing across the street. I shook his arm. "No, wait."

Wilfred nudged me with his elbow. We stepped down from the curbstone and took a few steps across Tompkins. Then the whole world seemed to explode: I was struck from the right by a fast-moving object that lifted me clear off the street.

The next thing I realized I was lying on the street, full length, on my right side with my arms flung wide.

"What on earth——" I found myself talking aloud and closed my lips. I tried to sit up erect but fell back when my head struck something hard and resistant above me. I put up my hand and felt long, heavy steel girders. These were much too high for an automobile; they must be the crossbars under a bus. But where was Wilfred? Had he been thrown clear, or was he, like myself, somewhere under the bus?

Instinctively I reached out with my hand and swung it across the surface of the paving in a wide arc. It touched clothing, which I knew must be Wilfred's. I edged along on my side until I could reach his hand. It was warm, lying quiet at his side. I picked it up and spelled into it, hoping that he had only been momentarily stunned by the fall. But there was no answering pressure from his fingers.

I decided to crawl out from under the bus to where I would be more likely to be seen by whoever was there. Feeling above my head, I noted the direction of the crossbeams and started to worm my way toward the side, still following one of them with my hand. To my horror, the bus began to move—at first slowly, then with gathering speed.

With a frantic effort, I rolled over and drew my arms and

legs into a tight huddle against my body. My heart pounded. "Oh, God!" I murmured. I must have repeated these two words several times before I became aware of the absence of the bus. A cold, light breeze fanned my face. I sat bolt upright and struggled to get to my feet. But suddenly I felt pain surging along my right knee—a searing pain that reminded me of the times I had banged my leg as a child against the sharp edge of a chair. I pushed downward with my hands and managed to climb to one knee; then I had to sit down again, unable to move.

Someone tapped my shoulder and bent over to say something; I could feel the whisper of breath against the lobe of my ear. I put out my hand and felt the heavy serge and metallic buttons of a policeman's uniform.

"Wait, don't talk to me that way—I'm deaf."

He reached into his pocket and thrust a pad and pencil into my hands.

"Oh no—not that. I can't see either. Please print in the palm of my hand—like this." I demonstrated what I meant, tracing a few letters across his palm. He understood.

"Where do you live?"

"Over at the Home, just a few steps away."

"Name?"

"Bob Smithdas."

"Can you get up?"

"I think I'll be able to move in a little while, just as soon as the pain stops."

Someone threw a blanket around me, and I drew the folds closer. It was cold sitting there all alone, and the stones under me seemed to be icy.

A few minutes later Eleanor, our cook, came to me and took my hand. I tried to read her lips, but my fingers had grown numb with cold; the pain in my leg distracted me with its constant throbbing.

She chafed my hand between hers. Then Vincent Smith, a member of the I.H.B. Staff, joined us. Vincent knew the manual alphabet and used it well. I managed to get to my feet with his help, standing unsteadily on one foot while I kept my weight from the other. Leaning on Vincent's shoulder, with Eleanor holding me by the waist, I limped over to a police patrol car. Vincent opened the door and lowered me into the seat.

I felt something warm touching my neck. I held my fingers in front of my face and sniffed. Blood.

We waited a few minutes; then the police driver opened the door and slid into the seat beside me. The car jerked forward and swung away from the corner. Within a few minutes we stopped at the Beth-David Hospital, not far from St. John's University.

Someone brought me a wheel chair; I dropped into it with a sigh. The exertion of walking, together with the nagging pain in my knee, had caused me to break into a cold sweat. I was wheeled rapidly down a hall heavily permeated with the odor of blended disinfectants and medicinal stuffs. Someone placed my hand on a padded table, and I understood that I was to get out of the chair and stretch out on it. Lying on the table felt more comfortable than sitting in the wheel chair, and the warm, heavily saturated air had a lulling effect upon me.

Firm fingers began to probe through my hair; they touched a sore area on the back of my scalp and stopped, parting the hair away from the cut. A blade began to scrape carefully but surely. I could barely feel the deft strokes as they made their short, quick way through the matted hair. But I knew the doctor was shaving the edges of the cut. After a little, there was the prickling sensation of a needle, and I realized that he was sewing sutures. I could feel the knots being tied and the loose ends being snipped away with a pair of shears.

After this I was taken to the X-ray room. Pictures were made of my head and leg injuries. It was decided that my knee must be operated on for the removal of cartilage. Before they wheeled me into the operating room I was quieted with a hypodermic needle and almost imperceptibly I began to sink into a fuzzy world of dreams. Vague figures kept moving through changing scenes; I dreamed that I heard voices and saw beautiful green countrysides.

When I awoke I found a nurse shaking me by the shoulder. My knee ached, so I put my hand down to hold it and discovered that my leg was in a solid cast. For several days I lay drugged with needles.

Then one afternoon my head cleared, the room stopped spinning. I was aware of someone approaching my bed. I reached up to feel the face of Father Docherty.

"How are you, Bob?"

I felt curiously detached as if I were still dreaming to the strains of invisible violins.

"I'm fine, Father. It's wonderful to see you."

The priest sat down and squeezed my hand. Almost imperceptibly I returned to the clear world of reality.

"Father, have you heard anything about Wilfred Couturier who was with me in the accident?"

For a moment he was silent. "He was killed by the bus, Bob. Let us be thankful he has been spared further suffering."

My throat tightened.

"How you survived, my boy, is a miracle. God was certainly with you."

"Father, I was wearing the medallion of the Virgin Mother

you gave me, when the accident occurred." I opened the top of my pajamas and showed my medal to him. "Remember what you said? 'This will take good care of you. Wear it always.' "

As Christmas drew near, I launched a campaign to get away from the hospital. Repetition, I knew, was the best medium for obtaining anything, so I continually asked the doctor when I could leave. I insisted that I would be just as safe at home as I would be here in the ward. Frankly I was worried about doing research for two of my term papers in philosophy. I would never be able to bring in the necessary pile of books I needed; the Braille volumes would take up too much space in the ward.

Eventually I won. One of the supervisors—a middle-aged woman with a jolly face and maternal personality—came over to my bed and said, "If you're a good boy, we might let you go back home on Christmas Eve. Behave yourself."

"Or my stockings will be filled with ashes and a bottle of sour beer," I added, remembering the old warnings we had been threatened with when we were children.

"Maybe." She patted my cheeks.

Sure enough, on Christmas Eve, after I had eaten my supper, John came to the hospital to take me home. It felt strange to be dressing myself again; my clothes had an unfamiliar tightness about them. I had not imagined how difficult it would be to put my shoes on. The cast on my right leg, reaching from the hip to just above my ankle, held my leg rigid so that I could barely reach my toes with my fingertips. But it felt wonderful to be standing up, fully dressed. We took the elevator to the main floor.

As I began to walk, the heavy plaster cast threw me off balance, so that I proceeded slowly with a listing to one side. Descending the short flight of steps to the street was a project. I had to go down holding onto the railing for support. "You're like an old man." John chuckled. "Old Pegleg."

Upon our arrival at the Home, John helped me upstairs to my room. Harry Weitman was delighted to see me; he threw his arms around my shoulders and gave me an affectionate hug. "Take it easy. You must be careful. I will help you with what you really need."

I hadn't realized that staying in bed could have such an effect on me; I felt tired and nauseated. With Harry's assistance I hobbled into my room and stretched out on my bed.

Harry came in to sit beside me.

"How do you feel?"

"All right. I'll feel better when I have a chance to walk around a little more."

Christmas Day passed quietly; it was enough for me to be at the Home, free to move about as I pleased, rather than being confined to a hospital. Hoping to recover as fast as nature would permit, I practiced walking about, even though the heavy cast proved to be a restrictive nuisance. Maude Mulvey, our matron, insisted that I stay in my room; she would bring my meals to me. After a day or two of being pampered, however, I became fretful. I decided to go down to the dining room alone, taking the stairs two at a time and swinging the cast in front of me. It was slow progress, but at least I could move with reasonable comfort.

In a month I was permitted to rejoin my classes at St. John's. The date was a red-letter one. John and I took the bus at the corner near the Home, then walked the three blocks to the college. It was a tiresome business to walk with one leg absolutely rigid, but it was even more tedious to climb three long flights of stairs to classrooms on the third floor. Sometimes, during the subsequent weeks, coming down the stairs, I would forget the cast and almost fall, but John kept a vigilant eye on me. Though I must have attracted a good deal of attention, I was happy that no one mentioned it to me.

In time, I really began to hate the cast. I took no special care of it, allowing it to bang into everything that happened to be in my way. Eventually the plaster over the knee began to soften. Then, one night while I slept, the cast broke in two. I woke up, wondering whether I should stay in bed or try to walk. I finally decided on the latter course, so I climbed out, slipped into a pair of sandals and stood up. I took a few steps. No pain whatever! I was so excited that I woke Harry, shaking him vigorously by the shoulder.

"Look!" I said, my fingers flying. "The cast is broken!"

Harry was alarmed. He sat up in bed, swung his legs over the side, and examined the cast carefully.

He scolded. "That is very bad. You should be more careful what the doctor said to do. How can we fix it?"

He finally hit upon a plan. He went to his bureau and produced two rolls of adhesive tape. He ordered me to climb back into bed, then fitted the two halves carefully together and wound the tape about the break several times.

The following morning Louis Bettica, who had succeeded his brother as head of the deaf-blind division, took me to the hospital.

"They'll have to put on a new cast."

"Nonsense!" I countered. "I don't feel any pain. Take it off and let me walk without it."

After bickering with the doctor for ten minutes, he finally assented. Nothing gave me more pleasure than to feel the ripping sound of the saw cutting the blasted thing away. But when I stood up I found that the sudden lessening of weight, together with the shrunken thinness of my leg, threw me out of balance. Still, I was able to walk slowly without too much difficulty. I was given a cane and hobbled happily out of his office.

Throughout it all, indeed from the moment I regained consciousness after the bus accident, I had tried my level best to live up to the teachings of that wise old poet, Horace: "A sense of humor is the best sauce for adversity."

It was due largely to God's mercy that the day arrived toward which my entire schooling had been pointing, my graduation from college.

During my last two years at St. John's my studies had become increasingly complex. My final term, as a matter of fact, was the most difficult I faced. At the beginning of the term I had been called into Dean Meyer's office, and something—call it presentiment—had warned me that trouble was in the offing.

"How many subjects are you carrying this term, Bob?"

"Four, Father—history of philosophy, English literature, government, and one other."

"I'm afraid you'll have to take two more. You do not have quite enough credits for graduation. In addition, we want you to write a biography to be submitted to the head of the literature department. Fortunately, we have decided to accept your credits from Michigan at their full value. I know you will be able to do the job if you really set to work."

There was no use in arguing, I knew; Father Meyer, in matters of directing a student on the path of learning, was absolutely immovable. I left the office, staggered by the amount of work I had been given.

"Now what?" I asked John. "I never dreamed I'd run into anything like this; I thought we were right along with the other fellows in credits. How did we ever get into this sort of predicament?"

"There's nothing you can do about it. You'll just have to take two more electives."

"Oh, nuts! It's all right for you to be complacent; I'm the one who's jinxed."

At home we picked up the catalogue of courses and looked through it for the two easiest and most interesting ones—courses which would fit my time schedule of classes. All the ones which appealed to me were in the wrong category, as far as time was concerned. Finally we decided to register for one course in the history of the Far East and another in political science.

The grind began almost immediately. I read continuously at night after I returned from my afternoon classes. During the first week of study I was assigned to write no less than six term papers, all to be finished before the mid-term tests were due. To make matters even worse, the course on history of the Far East turned out to be a gander. The text we used was crammed with obscure facts, and the professor, a Frenchman with an unpronounceable name, gave lectures which read like calendars—dates, dates, dates! It was difficult enough to remember the odd oriental names without having to associate them with definite places and times.

"Why didn't we check this sort of thing before it happened?" I moaned one afternoon in an outburst of frustration.

"Cheer up, Bob," Mr. Keane advised, "this happens to every student at one time or another."

"Not to the ones who know better."

He shook my hand with that gentle, friendly way he always had when he was trying to cheer me up. "Don't worry. Everything will turn out just as we planned it."

I had no answer to give him. I felt a genuine uplift of morale. When people believe in you, you can move mountains.

Another worry was where I would find all the reference books to use for my term papers. Eventually, by writing to various libraries, I managed to collect a pile of references, stacking the volumes six feet high in Lou Bettica's office.

I breathed a sigh of relief when I learned that I had kept my place on the honor list at mid-terms, but there was a nagging feeling that the finals would be the supreme test. "I've passed one hurdle," I said to John, "but I can always fall down at the last minute. So far, I've made every honor list to date; now you'll see me founder."

Before I realized it, there were only a few days left before the final exams—hectic days filled with studying and completing the final pages of essays. My favorite quotation now was one from the *Ode on a Grecian Urn* by John Keats. I must have recited it a score of times to John as we walked to school:

> "Who are these coming to the sacrifice?
> To what green altar, O mysterious priest,
> Lead'st thou that heifer lowing at the skies,
> And all her silken flanks with garlands drest?"

"Come on, cowboy," John would remonstrate. "You'll get there all the same."

Circumstances were kind to me. My professor of Far East history announced that if we handed in our essays promptly on the last Friday of the term, he would select the five best ones and exempt their authors from final exams. Filled with rising hope, I finished my essay in good time, only to be informed by John a few days prior to the deadline that the pages were all blank! "Your ribbon must have faded out," he announced. "We'll have to get a new one on that typewriter of yours."

Writing hurriedly, chiefly by memory and with a few hasty references to my books, I managed to have the paper ready for Friday, although I had had to spend most of the previous night completing it. My confidence was gone; the essay sounded desultory to me after the sleeplessness of the previous hours.

My relief was substantial when, on the following Monday as he had promised, the professor announced the names of those who would be exempted. I was one of them. I said a little prayer of thanksgiving.

The morning of my final session with examinations Lou Bettica and I walked home together. The sunshine was strong, and under the trees, near the park it smelled dusty and dry and clear. I hadn't slept well for the past two weeks, and the burden of relief was so great I could scarcely express it. But I felt nostalgic, too. Four years is a long time, and I had come to look upon St. John's with tenderness. I kept recalling the rickety creak of the old floors, the worn treads of the stairs that had been pounded by thousands of students' feet, the bulletin board that John and I had consulted nearly every morning, the cafeteria where we had taken our coffee and eaten lunch time after time. Colleges always seem to have some special, personal atmosphere about them; they are like old friends, growing grayer and friendlier with the years.

Lou and I stopped at a small lunchroom for a dish of spaghetti. We sat down in the stiff, straight backed chairs at a table with an oilcloth cover.

"Well, how does it feel to be finished with school, Bob?"

"I don't really know. After all the experiences I've had, I'll miss it."

When the results of the exams were announced I was gratified to learn that I had continued my high marks. As a matter of fact, I was scheduled to graduate with honors (*cum laude*) within the upper 10 per cent of the class, on a 90.2-per-cent average.

That day of my final exam, still excited over my release from pedagogy, I hurried in to see Mr. Keane at the Home. "All finished," I announced as soon as I was sure he had put down the phone he was holding. "My college days are over."

"Well, now; congratulations! We've been waiting for this day a long time, Bob. Now I can get to work and plan a little party for you. As a matter of fact, I've been planning it all along, and Mr. Salmon is just as enthused as I am. Do you think your folks will come up to New York if we invite them?"

"Of course! Dad has been hoping for this graduation for years; and all my sisters will come too. But that would be rather expensive for the Home—having so many people attend a party. Perhaps we ought to forget about it; we could just have a little gathering."

"Don't be modest, Bob. This is something special. Just leave it to me. Send me a list of all the people you would like to have invited, and I'll take care of the rest."

The story of the completion of my studies at St. John's inevitably made its way into the New York newspapers. I was alarmed; publicity was an entirely new aspect of the subject; I had not supposed that I would become, quite suddenly, the focal point for reporters and photographers. One afternoon Mr. Keane called me in.

"Now that you're a young celebrity, Bob, you'll have to live it down. You and Johnny are to appear on Chuck

Trainer's television program one night this week, so I'll give you a little coaching beforehand."

"Wait. I've never been on television. I have no experience in that field."

"Never mind. It will be easy enough. Father Docherty will be with you, since the program was arranged through St. John's."

"What shall I talk about?" I demanded, far from comfortable at the thought of being viewed by millions of people.

"Yourself. Your studies at St. John's."

"Talking about myself is a hopeless subject. I've done nothing unusual."

"You may think it's ordinary, Bob, but there are many who will consider it extraordinary."

John and I met Father Docherty at the studio in the evening, a few hours before the program was scheduled to go on the air. Chuck Trainer turned out to be a tall, husky young man with a pleasing personality; he made us feel at home immediately, he was so outright and friendly about the show.

"I'm not going to give you any script to memorize," he told me. It was easy to read his resonant voice. "But I do want you to feel that you are among friends. These people we are going to speak to are just ordinary Americans like all of us; they don't know your story, so tell it as simply as you can. Just relax—that's the important thing."

"But what happens if I become confused?" I asked. "Suppose John isn't able to follow the program with the manual alphabet?"

"We'll take care of that. If there's any confusion, I'll be here to handle it. If you really want to have something to remember so that you won't be flustered later, I'll give you a few leading questions."

Still, I had a deep-seated feeling of misgiving. It was all too new, and the idea of television had never entered my mind.

The time came for the opening commercial. The overhead lights came on; it grew unbelievably hot. Outside, the night was heavy and warm; here under the floodlights the heat reminded me of a broiling day in the middle of summer. Drops of perspiration rolled down my brow, and my white shirt felt like a wet tent. But to my surprise, everything went smoothly —the questions and answers, the light stories we had planned to tell the audience. Father Docherty took the brunt of the show, handling it, as John later pointed out, like an old master. And when it was over, Father commented jokingly, "I never thought I would be associated with a television star!"

"Quit pulling my leg, Father," I rejoined. "If anyone was a star, it was probably yourself. John and I must have looked extinguished."

A day later Mr. Keane called us back again, this time to tell us of another television appearance.

"This is going to be a big show," he explained. "We want you to give us the names of the people who have meant most to you; people who have really helped you on the way up. Now I've already talked to your family. Of course, Father Docherty will be another if he has the time to spare. But what about your teachers at the Pittsburgh school and Perkins?"

"What kind of show is this?" I inquired.

"It's called *We, the People*. They want to dramatize your story, so we'll have to get a few of your friends together. Think it over and bring me a list this afternoon."

The name of the program was vaguely familiar; I had read somewhere that it was one of the most prominent shows on television. I went to the office, sat down at a Braille writer, and began to work out a list of names. It seemed a hopeless task, so many people had come into my life, and all of them had left some real influence behind. The final list of names ran to more than twenty persons.

"What! You've given me too many names!" Mr. Keane protested when I brought the list to him. "The show is only an hour long; you'll only be on the air for about twenty minutes, and here you've given me enough for a lifetime."

"Isn't it a life story?"

"Well, certainly, but we'll have to boil the names down to just a few. Which of your teachers do you think had the most influence on you during your school days?"

"Miss Hunt at the Pittsburgh school, I think; and then there are Miss Nilsson, Miss Carpenter, and Mr. Jablonske at Perkins."

"Let me think. I'll let you know as soon as I can who will be coming up for the program."

It finally resolved itself into a small group: family, Miss Nilsson, Lou Bettica, Johnny, and myself. When I heard the names, I was disappointed; Miss Carpenter and Mr. Keane were not among them.

"You've left out two of the best," I protested when Mr. Keane had finished. "Where is Miss Carpenter's name? And your own?"

"Miss Carpenter can't leave her classes at Perkins right now—she's in the middle of graduation exercises. And I won't be there, either."

"Why not? You've always been the one who has given me advice and guidance. You can't do this sort of thing." I was glum with disappointment.

"Never mind me, Bob. I don't think you'll need me there."

"Please come, Mr. Keane—you know it's something special. I want you to be a part of it."

"There just isn't any chance of it. I'm needed here, and you know that I never like getting into the limelight. Maybe some other time, Bob."

I realized that he was adamant; there was no use in arguing with him. Nevertheless I felt frustrated and disappointed. I wanted this courageous man to be part of the story he had helped to make possible during the past four years. It was only right and proper, and when I thought of all the help he had given me I was overwhelmed. But, as Johnny said, there was nothing to be done.

It was wonderful to see my family and friends gathered together in my father's hotel suite on the night before the show was scheduled. Father and my sisters—Olga, Lil, and Ruth; my two brothers-in-law, Mike and Joe; Miss Hunt; Miss Nilsson; Father Docherty; Lou Bettica and Johnny and myself. It was a gay evening, full of warm friendliness and good fellowship. Everyone was happy, and I was the happiest of them all. Dad sat in an armchair in a conspicuous place, sitting up with his shoulders thrown back and a wide smile on his face.

"What are you grinning about?" I asked him teasingly. "You look like the cat that swallowed the canary."

"Why not? You're my son and a college boy. I never thought I'd live to see it happen—the only one of my children to go to college, and you who can't see or hear."

I felt embarrassed by this expression of pride. "Forget it, Dad. You know very well that you and Mother always believed I could do it."

He reached up and put an affectionate hand on my shoulder.

I went over and sat down on the edge of the chair where my sister Olga was. Olga was always quiet in her sweet way; I knew she wouldn't say anything to make me feel uncomfortable. "How do you feel about it?" Olga asked.

"About what?"

"Graduating."

"I'm glad, of course. But I don't think there should be such a fuss over it. Dad is all excited."

"Yes. You'd think he was the one who graduated."

It was after midnight when the party broke up. No one seemed willing to leave, yet all of us realized that there was a long day ahead at the studio.

The following morning we all met in Radio City shortly after noon. John Seymour, in charge of the show, immediately began the process of drilling us on our scripts. Since I was the only one who couldn't read, I had to memorize mine—just a few words explaining what I intended to do when I finished my training, and an expression of thanks to all those who had helped me. We spent the entire afternoon, with the exception of time out for lunch and dinner, running through the show, timing it for precision. All of us were nervous.

When the program went on the air John and I stood in the background waiting for our cues. One by one the others went under the bright lights and the cameras.

"Your Dad has tears in his eyes," John reported. "He's doing a grand job. And there's pride in his voice, too—it's so thick you could cut it with a knife."

My own turn came. John and I moved in beside John Seymour at the microphone. While John was talking and Mr. Seymour was making comments I tried to recall the part I had memorized, but it vanished into thin air. I wished fervently that I could see the big cards on the wall that the others had been using. Finally John nudged me, and I slipped my hand up to read Mr. Seymour's lips.

"And what are you planning to do now, Bob?"

Quick—quick! I had to say something. Improvise.

"I hope to continue working at the Industrial Home for the Blind in Brooklyn. I'd like to become an instructor for the blind and deaf-blind. And I want to thank all my friends who have helped me—my family, my teachers and all of them."

I stepped back, turned around, and met Ruth. It had been arranged that we were to kiss each other, so I bent forward. As our faces met, I noticed that Ruth's cheek was wet; I realized that she was crying silently. I pinched her.

"No dramatics," I whispered. "Wait till we're out of this."

The show ended. Seymour ran off to the monitor room and came back in a moment. He gripped my hand and said, enthusiastically, "Fine job, Bob. It was a pleasure."

Everyone seemed excited; everyone kept commenting on the program. Olga, who had been watching one of the screens, told me, "Ruth looked beautiful on the show—her eyes were like stars. And you should have seen Dad! He was just like a professional!"

Happiness is such an inexpressible thing. When you have too much of it, there never seems to be any way to put it into words. I was proud of all of these people; they had been the milestones of my life, the people I had come to know and love.

Graduation Day was set for Sunday, and the day dawned breathless and hot. By noon the temperature was soaring into the nineties. John helped me into my cap and gown and we took a taxi to the Armory, where the ceremonies were to be held. The family, leaving from their hotel, had gone in through another entrance. John and I found the assembly area of my graduating class.

The march began. Class by class we moved into the auditorium and filed to our seats. There was a brief invocation by a bishop, then a speech by Dean Meyer. As each baccalaureate and other degrees were mentioned, the classes rose to their feet. This was the largest graduation St. John's had ever had; there were over a thousand graduates present. Then my name was called. It had been decided that Dean Meyer would present me with my diploma as a special event, so John and I wedged our way through the crowded row to the aisle and walked slowly up to the stage. We climbed the steps and stood beside the dean.

"He's reading something," John told me. "It's a special blessing from Pope Pius XII in Rome. He has sent you his special Apostolic Benediction. Father Meyer is reading it now to the gathering. Put out your hand. Father Meyer is ready to give you the diploma and the Pope's personal blessing."

I reached out and took the roll of sheepskin. Father Meyer grasped my hand warmly. Suddenly I became aware of a new sound: the stage was vibrating, trembling. It seemed to go on and on.

Father Meyer patted my shoulder and John and I moved slowly back to our seats. When we were seated again I asked him about the unusual stir.

"They gave you a tremendous ovation. Really tremendous. I've never heard anything like it in all my days. Couldn't you feel the stage trembling?"

I nodded but said nothing. I was too happy.

Later the Pope's commendation was read to me in detail by Johnny:

June 11, 1950

My dear Mr. Robert Smithdas:

I am pleased to inform you that on the occasion of your graduation from St. John's University in Brooklyn with the Degree of Bachelor of Arts, our Most Holy Father, Pope Pius XII, has very graciously deigned to bestow upon you his special Apostolic Benediction. This Blessing is granted as a token of the paternal affection of His Holiness in recognition of your splendid achievements despite physical handicaps and as a pledge of heavenly favors for the years which lie ahead.

It is the express wish of the Sovereign Pontiff that this Blessing be shared by your father, by Mr. John J. Spainer, by your teachers and classmates and by all your relatives and friends who join with you in celebrating this joyous graduation day.

While conveying to you this august message of the Vicar of Christ I wish to add my own personal congratulations and good wishes.

With sentiments of esteem and with renewed felicitations, I remain

> Sincerely yours in Christ,
> S. G. Casgnani
> Archbishop of Laodicea
> Apostolic Delegate

After the graduation ceremonies we met the family outside the gates of the Armory. Father suggested that we have dinner at the St. George Hotel, so we took a taxi downtown. When we arrived we had several tables put together to form one long table for all of us. Dad ordered a toast. "This is my treat," he announced. "It only happens to me once in a lifetime."

Dinner was wonderful: we ate and talked for nearly three hours, all of us gay and excited. An orchestra was playing on a dais at the end of the dance floor; Ruth asked me to dance, so we moved out to the floor.

At first it was difficult; we kept colliding with other couples. Then the crowd thinned.

"Where has everyone gone?" I asked wonderingly.

"We're the only ones dancing," Ruth answered, using lip reading because we were in motion. "They've turned the spotlight on us."

"Good heavens! How did that happen?" I fell out of step and Ruth squeezed my arm.

"Don't be excited; follow me. Everyone is watching."

I felt trapped. I hadn't expected anything like this to happen. But I realized I had to dance as well as I could.

The following day I went to Mr. Keane for final information about a reception and party he had planned for the following evening. The events of the past few days had come so riotously that I was living in a world of perpetual motion.

"When are we going to finish this? It goes on and on forever."

"It will all be over by tomorrow," he said reassuringly. "You have just one more fling before the end. Now about this party we're having. There will be your family and John's family, and your friends. In addition, Mrs. Stone will bring a number of her Braille transcribers—the ladies who helped prepare your textbooks. We will also have Mr. Barnett from the American Foundation for the Blind and a few of his staff, Mr. Herbert Brown of the New York State Vocational Rehabilitation Service and some of his staff, as well as Mr. Wills, Mr. Conover, and other members of our own Board of Trustees. There will be a group of about two hundred people at the clubhouse of the Home."

"And what do I do?"

"Well, we're going to present you and Johnny with two gold watches. You'll be expected to make a little speech, to thank all those people for their help."

"I hope I won't forget anyone. Is there anything else?"

"Yes, we've arranged to have a few congratulatory messages read to the people. I think that will top everything off."

We had all agreed that we would spend the afternoon of the party resting from the exertions of the previous evening; but instead of relaxing, I spent most of the time trying to plot an acceptable speech. Nothing I could think of seemed adequate; either the tone was too formal or else I felt it wasn't sincere enough. As time waned, I became more irritated.

"What can I say?" I asked John mournfully. "Nothing seems just right, and this is an important occasion for me."

"Don't worry about it," he replied in his usual quiet way. "Just thank them all. Tell them from your heart—that will be the easiest way."

I was inclined to agree, so I gave up my fruitless search for words. I went to my room and lay down, intending to rest a while before I dressed for the night. I fell asleep.

John woke me up an hour before it was time to leave. When we arrived at the clubhouse we found it crowded with people, a number of whom were familiar, some of whom I had never met but had read about from time to time. I was bewildered by the ceremony of shaking hands, the names John kept giving me, and the friendly greetings of newcomers who were total strangers to me. Indeed, I was so confused that it was a relief when John finally led me to my seat at the head table.

"They have everything done up in real style," he told me. "The flower decorations are beautiful—roses, gladioli, carnations and some other flowers I can't name. Look." He passed my hand over the table array—ribbons, baskets, flowers everywhere. The air was heavy with the sweet, elusive fragrance of freshly cut blooms.

The dinner was a delicious one, and for dessert, apropos of the occasion, we had ice cream carved out in the shape of little boys sporting graduation caps and gowns. I was glad to concentrate on my food; it took my mind away from the moment when I would have to address the guests.

Then Mr. Salmon, acting as master of ceremonies, began to speak. He told the story of my past five years at the I.H.B., how I had been trained in its workshops, how they had decided to sponsor me at St. John's. He finished with a eulogy which made me wonder if I deserved it; surely the credit for my achievement, I knew, belonged to others, many of whom were present. Then he turned the evening over to Mr. Wills, president of our Board of Trustees.

Mr. Wills read messages that had been sent to me, and no one could have been more surprised than I to learn who had sent them. A beautiful tribute came from Helen Keller, congratulating me on being the only deaf-blind individual to graduate from college since her own achievement, fifty years before. There was also a message of congratulations from the mayor of New York, William O'Dwyer, and one from Governor Thomas E. Dewey. But the message that interested me most was one from President Harry S. Truman. I was truly startled; I had not dreamed that the President of the United States would send me a personal message. It was staggering.

"If this keeps up," John whispered, "I'll have to buy you a new hat—size fifteen."

I was pleased when Mr. Salmon asked my father to bow to the guests. Father, a little tremulous with excitement,

"It sounds interesting, but I've never had any experience."

"Well, I think it might work. Suppose you write out a speech—say for about two minutes—and let me mull it over. Then we'll see."

Inability to hear myself speak has been a constant problem. Perhaps no one has been more conscious of this than Mr. Keane, who has always been my best counselor and friend during the years I have been in Brooklyn. He has never been satisfied with my progress; and always, in our conversations together, he has endeavored to point out various ways for me to improve myself. "We'll have to polish the rough diamond a little more." It was Mr. Keane who suggested that I have speech-correction lessons during my summer courses in Michigan.

But the most intensive training in speech that I have ever had was with a professional singer, John di Francesco. John, who had also attended Perkins while I was there, had studied under Ezio Pinza, the Metropolitan Opera's great basso. When Mr. Keane told me that he had arranged for him to give me lessons, I was puzzled.

"But, Mr. Keane, John is totally blind! I don't see how he will be able to watch the movements of my lips and tongue while I am forming sounds."

"Well, we'll chance that. It will be an experiment for both of you, I think. But there is one thing that concerns me; I feel that you are not getting as much power into your voice as you should. I can't express it exactly, but I feel that you use too much breath in making certain sounds, so that you have something like an aspirate quality to your speech. Now, don't misunderstand me, Bob—I think your speech is far more articulate than many people's utterances. Still, we can improve it somehow."

John di Francesco was far more adequate than I had

thought; he seemed to know exactly what I was doing with my facial muscles, my throat and diaphragm. He taught me to control my breathing through practice drills in holding vowel sounds or sustained consonants for extended intervals.

"Bob, I want you to remember that vocal sound is the result of the interaction of breath and vocal chords. A proper balance must be maintained between the action of the breath and the reaction of the vocal chords; the breath must be sufficiently concentrated and the vocal chords sufficiently resistant to result in firm sound, at whatever dynamic level desired. However, there should be no constriction in the neck, face, throat or tongue."

John evolved lists of words with sustained vowels and sustained consonants, and I practiced these whenever I had a free hour. We communicated through the medium of lip reading so that I had ample time to observe exactly how speech was formed naturally and effectively. When the lessons came to an end at the beginning of summer I felt a twinge of regret, for I had thoroughly enjoyed working with John. He was never impatient, and the encouragement he gave me was invaluable. In consequence of his teaching, I felt more relaxed in my speaking engagements.

My debut as a public speaker was at one of the junior high schools in lower Manhattan.

I had gone in to see Mr. Keane the previous Monday morning. I found him sitting behind his desk, leaning back in his swivel chair, and with the omnipresent telephone drawn up in front of him. I sighed when I noticed the telephone; I knew I would have to wait until the incoming call was finished, and it was more than likely that he would pick it up again before I could even begin to report to him on my progress.

When he finally hung up he turned to me with satisfaction.

"How is the new lecturer today? I have a bit of news for you and John, and I think you'll like it. Tomorrow at two o'clock both of you will be speaking at one of the public schools over in Manhattan. It's not a regular assembly—just a class of older students—but I think you'll find it interesting."

"On such short notice? Why we've hardly begun to assimilate all that material you gave us about the Home's history, our philosophy of blindness, and the rest. John and I haven't even practiced our speeches yet."

"Cheer up, my lad. You don't need to practice; I feel that if you just talk from the cuff, you'll be more spontaneous. I don't want you to sound like a broken record. Of course, I know there will be mistakes in the beginning, but we expect that anyway. What I want you to remember is that you and John are to give these kids a picture of what our blind people can do if they have the opportunities they need. We want them to know that blind people are just plain citizens like everyone else. Do you understand?"

John and I arranged a hasty outline of the program, and though neither of us seemed certain of our aims, we at least agreed upon the bare essentials of how to proceed. John would introduce me, give a short biographical sketch of my life, and then turn the program over to me. Then I would give a short account of the history of our service program, and continue with an illustration of how many of our blind people were a credit to their neighbors and the communities in which they lived. A motion picture showing the various phases of our work would follow; then, if there was still time enough, we would go into a question and answer period.

During the opening exercises I tried to recollect the main

points of the speech I had planned for the group. My mind became utterly confused.

"What's the matter, old boy?" John inquired. "Do you have stage fright?"

"I don't know what you mean, but if it's anything comparable to what I feel now, I have a jolly good case of it. How much longer will we have to wait?"

"Not too long. The teacher in charge is introducing me now."

When John stood up and moved to the front of the room I began to fidget with one of the buttons on my sleeve. I caught myself mumbling under my breath, then began playing a game of twiddle-thumbs, rotating my thumbs in opposite directions.

John came back and led me to the center of the room. "Not too loud—medium voice," he cautioned. "Give them the works, old boy."

In spite of myself, I grinned. I was surprised to discover how easily I remembered the talk I had been practicing; the words came almost involuntarily, so that I soon regained my old confidence.

When I finished my talk John escorted me back to my seat, where I dropped down with an audible sigh. Turning to John, I asked, "Was it all right?"

"Well, your voice seemed a trifle high-pitched to me. But that's probably because you were nervous. And you turned a little too much to the right."

"What do you mean—turned to the right?"

"You kept moving gradually toward your right—just a little at a time. When you finished you were completely turned away from the audience. Next time, though, I'll try to put you in front of a table or beside something you can lay your hand on for direction."

I accepted these criticisms at face value, knowing that John was being absolutely honest in his commentary. Quite naturally, however, I was somewhat disconcerted and felt uncomfortable. Eager to improve myself, I insisted that John inform me whenever I had the least error in my speech or permitted myself to fall into any idiosyncrasy that would be obvious to the listening group. He gave me his assurance that he would, even if he thought it would disturb me.

We developed a system of signals so that John could give me directions while I was addressing my audience. Habitually, John would give me an idea of the size of the room, the number of people in the group, and the kind of acoustics, so that I could gauge my speaking range. If the room was small and intimate, he would tell me to speak with normal voice; if it was large, noisy, or the acoustics were poor, he would direct me to speak "half loud" or "very loud." Occasionally, when we were in an especially large auditorium, he would tell me, "This place is huge; high ceiling, deep and wide! You'll have to scream. And there is a balcony, too. Scream, brother, scream!"

If I began my lecture too softly, John would run his finger upward along my side to indicate that I needed to use more vocal power; and if I spoke too loudly, he would signal by moving his finger downward. There were times, too, when we were limited in speaking time, and then he would tell me that I had two minutes left in which to finish my talk, simply by tapping me twice. Fortunately for me, these signals rarely had to be repeated; I seemed able to keep my voice at a given volume once I had begun to speak, and somehow—perhaps automatically—I was able to recognize the length of the time I was speaking.

"You must have a built-in volume control and time clock," John wisecracked.

As our first year of programing progressed, I gradually corrected any peculiarities that occurred during my public appearances. John would point them out to me and make suggestions, and I would follow them through. As I learned to be more relaxed, my tendency to sway on my feet lessened until it ceased entirely. My voice, which was naturally soft and untrained, became more resonant and powerful.

During the middle of the year Niles and Elaine Welch joined the Special Education and Information Staff of the I.H.B. and gave me additional instruction in lecturing techniques. Niles Welch had been a screen and television actor and a senior announcer of the Columbia Broadcasting System. During the war he became an official of the Voice of America, producing programs on the American way of life for the State Department. Upon completing a broadcast in 1945, Niles bumped into a studio door accidentally, suffered a detachment of the retina of both eyes, and went blind.

This tragedy brought Niles Welch to the attention of the I.H.B. Soon after Niles was hired, Elaine, his wife, who had been a Broadway actress, joined the staff. They worked together as a team to further develop in me a sense of platform presence. Thanks to the Welches, I am today quite busy on the lecture platform.

It did not take long for me to realize how little my audiences knew about blind persons. During the question and answer periods following the programs I found that it was not unusual to hear the same questions repeated over and over again. Could blind people really hold jobs and support themselves? How could I shave and dress myself? Did someone feed me, or did I eat like other people? Did all sightless people have guides?

To anyone fully informed about the problems of blindness, such attitudes seem amusing. I soon realized how un-

familiar most people were with the idea of anyone losing
his sight and remaining a normal human being. They wanted
to know, to believe, that losing one's sight did not necessarily
change one's attitude toward life; they wanted to be reassured
that his mysterious absence of vision—a state which they
inevitably pictured as complete darkness and isolation—could
be surmounted by initiative.

I have always tried to give my listeners a realistic summary
of what some of our sightless people have achieved, and I
have made it a point to keep the story untainted by any
emotional value which might arouse pity.

There was the young boy in a high-school assembly who,
after one program was completed, came to the stage and said:
"I've always thought of becoming a minister, but now I'm
sure I should be one."

And there was the little girl who came to me after an
assembly and handed me a handful of pennies. "I want you
to have this." (John commented that he had never seen such
a solemn little face.) "It's all I've got, but if I had more, I'd
give it to you to help someone who can't see."

There have also been sincere souls—mostly women—who
have been so deeply moved that they have burst into tears.
Such sentimentalism has always made me feel uncomfortable. The first time it happened, I turned to John and whispered, "What on earth have I said that would cause so much
grief? I thought I gave them a rather bright picture of our
work."

Public speakers are prey to many curious situations. There
are moments of unaccountable excitement, discouragement,
humour. It was at a meeting of Rotarians one day when
during the question and answer period following the showing
of our film, *Eve of Life*, some people around me burst into
laughter.

"Now what's happened?" I asked one of them.

"It is hilarious," I was told. "When it was mentioned that you had earned your master's degree from New York University, one of the members of the audience dropped his false teeth in amazement."

I still recall our appointment with a Democratic women's club in Far Rockaway, Long Island. The meeting was scheduled to be held in the local firehouse, but when we arrived we were told that the group had moved to other quarters a few streets away. We followed the address we were given and discovered that the Democrats had moved to still another place. When we traced them to the third address the chairwoman declared that the person who had made the arrangements had abruptly left the club to become a Republican!

Once we drove out to Rockaway to attend the meeting of a women's group. As we walked into the building, I was told that I was to meet a Mrs. Klineman.

"Very pleased to meet you, Mrs. Klineman." I put out my hand.

People around me began to chuckle. "Do you know, Bob, she thought that *you* were leading your attendant."

Forgetfulness of the fact that I am deaf as well as blind is often confusing. On occasions when I have been left alone for a few moments, a member has walked up, grabbed my hand in a vigorous handclasp, and proceeded to shout at me. The best I can do under such circumstances is to reply, "It's nice to see you again."

Perhaps the most embarrassing occurrence took place at a Kiwanis dinner meeting. We were in Copiague, Long Island, and I somehow took it for granted that we were at the Copiague Lions meeting. Near the end of my speech I thanked the club for the interest they had shown in our program of services for the blind of Long Island.

"It's been a wonderful experience, knowing that the Lions have been so deeply interested in our work. We feel that the Lions have been instrumental in making our services available to a larger number of blind persons in the areas which we serve."

Suddenly I was nudged by David Windrow, my companion, and I dropped my hand to my side to see what was bothering him. "Kiwanis!" he spelled feverishly, "Kiwanis!"

I was profoundly taken aback, and yet I realized that if I showed confusion, the club would instantly recognize it. My mind flashed into action. Almost without a break, I continued:

"But if the Lions were first to help us in the field of service, the Kiwanis clubs were equally interested and responded with the same measure of spontaneity. With regard to our nursery-school children they have done a marvelous job in sponsoring many of the youngsters who need preliminary training before entering elementary school. . . ."

I do not recall the entire speech, but somehow I had managed a suave comeback.

After we had finished the evening and I walked to the car, a member of the I.H.B. staff came up. "Did you realize how graciously you pulled yourself out of that predicament, Bob?"

"But I actually thought it was a Lions Club. I felt so certain that I never for a moment doubted it."

"Well, anyway, it was wonderful the way you collected yourself and made the correction. Even the members commented about it; they were all very pleased that you could handle it so well."

"As a matter of note, I am surprised at myself. I haven't the slightest idea what I said—it's as blurred as a clouded sky."

Looking back in retrospect, it seems almost incredible that

in an average year I present 253 programs to groups totaling over 112,000 people. Recently, also, I have taken on another duty, serving as a consultant to the World Council of the Blind, an agency set up under the United Nations studying ways to establish an international system of communication for the deaf-blind.

I have always believed that one of the finest attributes of life is its quality of unexpectedness. The only reservation I have is that some of the surprises are not at all pleasant; sometimes they are quite tragic!

No one could have been more surprised than I when, two years ago last February, Johnny Spainer told me that he intended to enter the Army. We were having our afternoon coffee when he broached it. I had made a joking remark:

"You know, old boy, the Senate has just passed another draft quota for eighty thousand men. You're lucky your name isn't on the list."

There was a momentary pause, and then he said, "Maybe I'll go after all. It might be a good experience for me."

"What? You aren't serious?"

"I was never more serious in my life."

"But you're twenty-six—soon you'll be over the draft age. You haven't long to wait now. Why the sudden interest in army life?"

"I've been thinking about it for the past few months, Bob. I'm beginning to think it would be a nice change for both of us. Especially for you. It would give you something new to look forward to; you might enjoy the change."

"Nonsense! I'm quite satisfied to keep things as they are. I refuse to believe that you are serious at all."

"It's true enough. I am going to see Mr. Keane sometime this week; I'll ask him to find a new assistant for you. I've been thinking of sending in my application before spring so that I can go to camp during the warmer months. Honestly, Bob—I really have given it a lot of thought."

"What about your mother?" I was beginning to feel uncomfortable. "Who will take care of her? Your brother is married, and you're her only mainstay right now."

"Oh, she will make out all right—don't worry. I'll be sending her part of my monthly allowance, and she has a lot of friends whom she can visit while I'm away."

"I still don't believe it."

But a week later, when I had almost forgotten the matter, John told me he had spoken to Mr. Keane. Mr. Keane had—as I had guessed—tried to dissuade him, but John was adamant. He had also applied to the draft board for his physical examination.

"Since you've made up your mind, John, I suppose the best thing for me to do is be philosophical about it. I can see your point clearly enough. You are entitled to a change of scenery. When do you expect to leave?"

"I'll stay on until vacation time—I've asked the draft board to give me a stay until August. That will give you time to find someone to replace me."

"Nice, kind man. You know as well as anyone that no one will replace you."

"You'll get used to the new setup soon enough. It will be the best thing that ever happened to you."

"Nine years. That's a long time to be associated with another person. I feel damned blue."

"Cheer up, old man—I'll come to your wedding."

"Oh yes," I replied, smiling at the old joke between us. "I've promised to have you as my best man, and you agreed. A promise is a promise."

Nothing dissuaded John—nothing that I could say, or that

Mr. Keane or Mr. Salmon could put forward as arguments. There was nothing left for us to do except look for a new assistant.

It was past the beginning of May when we finally decided to place an advertisement in the New York newspapers. When we came into the main office one day, Mrs. Burns, our switchboard operator, dashed over to us. "No more advertising, please! The switchboards are jammed with calls." And they stayed jammed for two days as applicants called in to inquire about the opening in our public-relations office.

The applicant we finally selected was David Windrow, a cheerful young man with black hair trimmed in a crew cut that never seemed to be tamed, and a voluble way of talking. To my relief, he showed no signs of being ill at ease with me; on the contrary, he seemed quite capable of understanding the situation. He was the exact opposite of John: John was quiet, sometimes taciturn in his moods; David was as lively as a spaniel, inquisitive and unrestrained in his appraisal of life.

John immediately began teaching David the manual alphabet and the rudiments of Braille. Summer was coming; it was near the end of our speaking season, but we managed to include him in a few of the remaining programs so that he could have experience with our routine.

Near the end of June, Mr. Salmon announced the last staff meeting of the summer and dedicated it especially to John. All of the staff were fond of this quiet, dependable chap. But I doubt whether anyone guessed—except Mr. Keane and myself—how deeply moved he was by their display of affection. For my own part, as I stood up to present him with a personal gift, I felt an odd, choking sensation in my throat. All that came back to me was a blur of memories. "Nine years." The thought kept repeating itself like a revolving record. I remembered our fraternity parties when we had shared double dates; the summers in Michigan; the first programs we had presented together; and a thousand other incidents. Nothing seemed too trifling to remember.

Our last program was scheduled for the end of June in Batavia, New York, where we were to attend a meeting at the Batavia School for the Blind. We went up by train, and on the way I kept thinking, "This is the final program."

Neither of us said anything personal during the trip—not until we were on the night train speeding back to New York. The porter made up our berths and left the room. I was wide awake, even though it was nearly midnight, and John seemed equally restless. I sat down on the edge of the lower berth.

"It's odd, John, but do you realize that tomorrow will be the first of July—almost exactly nine years since we first met?"

"I hadn't thought of that, Bob, but you're right. Shall we have a drink, just to celebrate?"

"I thought you said there wasn't any club car on this train?"

"There isn't. But I bought some scotch before we left New York, just in case we might feel like having a little special session of our own." He dug into his suitcase and brought out the bottle. He filled two small paper cups with water and carefully poured the scotch.

"Here's to us." He tapped his drink against mine and took a long swallow.

"For auld lang syne." I touched the liquid to my lips.

"I hope you'll be back, John," I murmured. "I wonder what your years in the Army will mean to us."

"You'll keep yourself busy enough with your public speaking, your poetry, and your autobiography. I'm sure you'll get whatever you want, if you do anything about it."

"Do you remember what Wilde said in one of his plays—

243

that the two great tragedies of life are not getting what you want, and being able to get what you want?"

I opened the watch on my wrist and felt the circling hands. "It's three o'clock, and our train gets in to New York at eight. We had better turn in." I gulped down the remainder of my drink and threw the cup into one of the holders on the wall beneath the window.

As I pulled the blankets up around my shoulders and fixed the pillow comfortably behind my head, I kept thinking of the years John and I had been together. There had been moments when we had quarreled, of course; but the cheerful memories outweighed them. I had received a great deal of pleasure from my aquaintance with him, and I wondered whether I had given as much as I had received.

In the morning, at seven, the porter woke us. We dressed and shaved, and it was almost time for us to leave the train before we finished. We ate breakfast in a restaurant across the street from Grand Central. When the meal was finished we went outside and hailed a taxi.

Leaning back in my seat, I lit a cigarette. It had been decided that upon our arrival in New York, Ruth and my brother-in-law, Neal, were to pick me up at the Home and drive me to Pittsburgh for a few weeks' stay with my family. It was believed that this would make my period of adjustment easier.

"You'll enjoy yourself when you see your family again," John assured me as we rode home from the train. "Just think how happy they will be to see you."

"True enough. It's so pleasant to have a big family, and a lot of nieces and nephews."

"Paternal instinct." From the warm pressure of John's fingers, I knew he must be smiling.

When the taxi stopped in front of the Home on Gates

Avenue, we picked up the bags and hurried upstairs to my room. I dropped my small suitcase, the one I had taken to Batavia, under the table, then brought out a larger one for the trip to Pittsburgh. It was half full of my belongings; I hadn't had time to pack it the night before we left New York. John insisted on helping me finish.

We were still busy stuffing shirts and odds and ends into the bag when my brother-in-law arrived. Neal came into the room with his usual breezy air and pumped my hand up and down.

"Hurry up, I have to pick up Ruth as soon as we can get into New York."

Finally, by a rapid hit-and-miss procedure, John and I finished packing. John picked up the case, and we started down to the waiting Buick. As I climbed in, John gripped my hand.

"I guess this is good-by for a while, but I'll come to see you when I have the chance. Good luck, and take care of yourself."

"So long, soldier," I replied. I felt the old, tight feeling in my throat. I couldn't think of anything to say; and as the car moved smoothly out from the curb, all I could do was wave my hand through the open window.

Neal threw the car into gear and settled back in his seat. "Will you miss John? He's been with you a long time. Nice fellow."

"Certainly I'll miss him. He's been the most dependable, most trustworthy person I've ever known. But I suppose you have to let go sometime—you can't have such friends at your elbow forever. I hope he'll come back someday, but I'm afraid he won't. Life is full of changes."

As we drove along, the hot July sunshine streaming through the windshield, I began to feel more relaxed. The cloud of thoughts lifted. I began to concentrate on the three weeks of vacation before me; Dad and Olga and the children; my sister Lil and her family; and the old house on Sunnyland Street. It seemed ages since I had seen them. . . .

Certainly, with regard to my relationship with my new assistant, my experiences have undergone a change from the days of John Spainer. David Windrow is indeed different from John. He is much less reserved, much more impulsive. But the basic quality both have in common is their capacity for kindness.

I have always believed that one of the most compelling instincts of human nature is the desire to find a haven of intimate privacy where one can be entirely free to follow his own course of actions and where one can feel that he is master. Having lived the major part of my life in various schools for the blind, and at the residential home on Gates Avenue, I have felt an increasing need to put down my own roots, even though I realized that there might be difficult problems to face if I were to live alone. A home meant many things to me: a measure of personal independence in not being bound to the regulated life I had hitherto known; the reassurance that I could make my own decisions without criticism from others. But perhaps more than any other reason, it offered a new challenge to my ingenuity and resourcefulness. Would I be able to maintain a home and resolve all the problems it might entail because of my disabilities? Would I be able to solve the usual problems of domestic housekeeping—cooking, cleaning, buying supplies for an apartment—and act as a host when friends came to visit?

On several occasions I mentioned this project to members of my family, all of whom invariably tried to dissuade me.

They always thought of the same difficulties I had considered so many times, and their conviction that I would regret my foolhardy venture was unshakable.

"You'll starve!" my father said with emphasis. "Who's going to cook for you?"

"I will do my own cooking, Dad."

"You can't cook! And who will clean the place after you finish with it?"

"I'll do some of the house cleaning myself, of course; later I'll find a cleaning woman who can come in once a week. It will all work out—don't worry."

My sisters offered the same arguments. Olga was especially concerned, and she seemed appalled at the idea of my being alone in an apartment. "Why don't you find a nice girl and marry her?"

"Where? That sounds like a bigger order than moving into my own apartment!"

My sister Ruth shared Olga's feeling of concern, but her husband, Neal, considered the problem with more restraint. "It might be a good idea—you seem to want this more than anything else. Don't listen to the girls. If you are really set on this sort of thing, do what you think you want to do. It's your own business, Bob."

Mr. Keane seemed to be of the same opinion, though he also had some misgivings as to whether I would be able to meet the situation adequately.

"Well, Bob," he said, after he had listened to my newest venture, "the final decision will be yours. Of course you realize that there will be problems. If you need us, we will always be glad to help; but I think this project will be entirely up to you. I feel that your decision to move away from Gates Avenue shows that you are reaching a more mature outlook on life, and I know Mr. Salmon feels very much the same way."

And so I entered my application for an apartment at Clinton Hill, a housing development, overlooking Prospect Park in Brooklyn, which belonged to the Equitable Life Assurance Company. I had many reasons for selecting this particular location, but perhaps the most important one was that it was close to the bus route which shuttled between our main offices on Willoughby Street and the residential Home on Gates Avenue. Also, it was close to a shopping center where I could easily buy needed supplies.

Two weeks after I had applied I received notice that one of the apartments was vacant. I was overjoyed, but at the same time I was alarmed; I did not possess one piece of the necessary furniture! Furthermore, I signed the lease in early November, and the holiday season was close at hand.

I asked a good friend, Gerry De Angelis, whether he would help me furnish my apartment; I knew that his wife, Betty, had excellent taste, and I wanted my home to be not only comfortable but also attractive. We made arrangements to visit some of the better shops in New York during weekends. Betty, a charming girl, immediately began planning the layout of the rooms and the colors to be used.

We decided to furnish the living room in Danish modern, and the bedroom in the same style. Most of the furniture we selected was in dark walnut; the rest of the colors we chose carefully as we purchased each piece, and Betty insisted that everything must blend.

"We want something that fits your personality, Bob. The colors should be conservative and in good taste—not too light in shade."

We had the living room painted a pastel blue; the bedroom was done in green, and the kitchen and pantry in white.

Not being too familiar with color combinations, I left the choosing of materials and colors entirely to Betty. For the sofa she chose gold and beige; the armchairs were upholstered in chocolate, and the rug was cedar-colored. Shades of brown and gold ran through the entire apartment.

It was not until after the beginning of December that I moved to my new home. I was excited, of course, and I also felt a pang of misgiving. Had I been too rash in supposing that I could begin housekeeping on my own? Within a few days, however, my feeling of diffidence was gone; I began to enjoy the novelty of living alone.

David Windrow, who ordinarily acted as my attendant only on I.H.B. business, generously stayed with me during those first few hectic days while I was trying to orient myself and busily organizing the rooms. Not all of the furniture arrived at the same time, but there were the essentials: the bedroom, part of the living room, and the dinette.

We bought the staples I needed from the nearby supermarket. David showed me how to operate the gas range and the electrical equipment I had purchased during the preceding weeks. While he prepared our meals, I watched him carefully, noting everything that might be of value to me, for I still didn't know much about cooking.

Several days after I had moved into the apartment my sister Ruth came to visit me. She seemed excited and hurried from one room to another, checking every detail. In the kitchenette, she inspected the contents of the refrigerator and began throwing out some of my accumulated foodstuffs.

"What are you doing?" I asked, noticing that she was tossing several packages into the refuse bin. "You're throwing away all my food!"

"The next time you buy liver, use it the same day. Don't

keep it for a week. And your vegetables are getting moldy. Don't you have a vegetable tray?"

"I never thought of that."

"And look at those window sills! Don't you ever dust them?"

"Well, the cleaning woman hasn't come yet. I've tried to keep the apartment as shipshape as possible."

"You need a hamper in the bathroom, and little shades on those wall brackets. I'll find a nice rug for the dinette, too—something in black and gold."

David, when he heard about the rug for the dinette, seemed perturbed.

"Those floors are parquet; why cover them with a rug? They're beautiful by themselves."

"Ruth says I should have a rug to relieve the bareness. Besides, it won't cover the entire floor."

"I disagree about the rug entirely. But you should have some paintings for the walls in the living room. Not reproductions, though—something original."

"Where am I going to find original paintings?" I asked. "They would cost me a small fortune, and I've already invested too much in the furniture."

"Do you remember the artist I introduced you to a while ago? He's in the hospital, and he's very ill. He might be willing to sell two of his water colors at a reasonable price—he needs the money badly."

"What's the matter with him?"

"He has pneumonia, complicated by malnutrition."

David told me the story of the artist, a man who was fairly well known in America. He had never been willing to sell his paintings, which he regarded with almost maternal care; he was content to display them in art galleries, but nothing would induce him to sell them. Though he had come from a well-to-do family, he had squandered whatever money he had and during the last few years had been receiving welfare. "A tiger and her kittens are nothing compared to this fellow and his art," David said to me.

We went to visit the artist in the hospital. He seemed moved by my desire to buy two of his pictures. We could only stay with him for a few minutes, but we were rewarded when he finally agreed to permit me to choose from his paintings at an art gallery on Fifth Avenue.

The following day we went to the gallery to select the paintings. David described each one in detail; then I made my final selection—one called "Angel in the Woodland," and another called the "Rose Pavilion." David seemed pleased.

"I think you've chosen the two best paintings. They're romantic, and I believe they will go beautifully with your furniture. The coloring is just right."

My brother-in-law, Neal, whose brother was also a painter in his leisure time, was delighted with the paintings. "They're beautiful! When the room is all arranged, these will make it look perfect."

Just as we had anticipated, there were problems to be solved, and the solutions were not always forthcoming.

Since my apartment is on the eleventh floor of the building, I must use the elevator—and there are two elevators, both controlled by a single set of buttons. This is an awkward situation for me, since the two shafts are more than eight feet apart. After pressing the button to bring the elevator to my floor, I must walk back and forth between them until one of them arrives.

And once I am in the elevator, anyone on lower floors can stop it. Several times when other tenants have joined me in the elevator I have gotten off with them, only to discover that I was on the wrong floor! Then I noticed that the numbers of the floors were heavily painted on the doors of the shafts; by feeling the numerals I could determine what floor the elevator had reached.

The gas stove in my kitchenette also presented a problem —or, at least, we thought it was a problem. My friends were concerned because the gas used in New York is highly inflammable and ignites suddenly. Everyone seemed to feel that it would be too dangerous for me to use; Mr. Salmon even suggested that I use an electric stove instead. But there were no outlets for electric stoves; the house current was the usual one hundred ten volts, and a stove would require two hundred and twenty volts. Fortunately, the burners on my range—as in all modern gas stoves nowadays—were lit by a pilot light. But how to light the oven?

I remembered my experience, years before when I was still a small boy, when I had tried to light our oven at home and the gas had exploded, singeing my hair. I was reluctant to try the same experiment. Then David hit upon a plan; we bought a box of straws, lit one from the burners, turned on the oven, and slipped the straw underneath. It works beautifully, provided I am extremely careful.

Unaccustomed to the duties of housekeeping, I sometimes found myself so preoccupied with one particular chore that I completely forgot others. This led to disasters, as I discovered when I flooded my kitchenette.

I had just finished dinner one evening and, as usual, I planned to wash the dishes. I stacked the plates in the sink and turned on the water. Then I remembered that I had forgotten to put the butter back in the refrigerator. I went into the dinette to look for it; finally I found it on the window sill where I had absent-mindedly left it.

As I walked back to the kitchen I felt a peculiar sloshing

under my feet. The floor was flooded—I had forgotten to turn off the water! I spent the next half hour sponging diligently, thoroughly mortified that I had been so careless.

And then, one morning when David came in, I was interrupted at the same chore of dishwashing. I wanted to show him some new things I had bought, and while we were discussing them he suddenly turned around. "Water!" he exclaimed, and dashed into the kitchenette. Again I had forgotten to turn it off, and he had not realized that it was overflowing until he heard the steady drip, drip, behind him.

Because most of my friends are sighted, I realized that I would have to buy an adequate number of lamps to light my apartment when visitors came to see me. Gerry and Betty ordered three of them for the living room.

"You'll probably find them in your apartment on Monday," Gerry told me. "Just leave a note on the door to tell the delivery men that you are at home, and leave the door open. Pay them by check."

But the delivery came on Saturday while I was away visiting a friend. There was a note saying that they would be back on Monday.

On Monday there was no delivery; but while I was at the office the following Wednesday the lamps arrived—and were taken away again! David advised me to leave the check with the guard in the booth in the middle of the garden, and we left a hurried note on the door to direct the delivery men to him. On Friday they reappeared but with only two lamps; the guard refused to accept them, knowing that I expected three. He returned the check to David; and David, as confused as myself, finally decided to call the store the following day. And then, on Saturday, the three lamps were delivered! But since there was no check to pay for them, the men returned them to the store again.

No more deliveries were made; I got a card asking me to reorder, since the store had lost trace of the elusive lamps. However, I had no desire to continue chasing them about, so I finally asked Ruth and Neal to purchase lamps for me.

I planned to have a housewarming party for my friends on the staff, so toward the middle of January, though I had been a homemaker for less than two months, I began preparation. A friend of mine, Enid, came to set up the tables and see that everything was in readiness. One can scarcely imagine her dismay when, on the appointed day, she discovered that I had not yet received the tables or lamps for my living room.

"We need tables, and we need lamps! I thought you had already gotten them."

"I've been trying to get those things for weeks," I told her. "Tomorrow David is driving over to the main freight depot in New Jersey to pick up the tables. And the lamps—well, they haven't arrived yet. We'll have to borrow a few from David, I suppose."

"And where is the living-room rug?"

"Oh, that's coming tomorrow."

"What! Tomorrow? We're having your party tomorrow!"

"It would be just my luck if the rug was delivered in the middle of the party—just wait and see."

Enid had brought a friend, Kathleen Rice, with her, and while Kate and I polished silver, she busied herself with the cooking. Like most males, I felt peculiarly out of place; Enid and Kate took over so thoroughly that I had very little to do after I had finished polishing.

At noon the following day Enid came in to set out the table. She had not been with me more than half an hour when the door opened and the delivery men brought in the Persian rug. It was enormous, and the men refused to lay it out.

"What will we do?" Enid asked.

"I guess we'll have to lay it ourselves."

"Maybe I can get the porter to do it."

"We'll wait for an eternity before he comes up. We had better do it now."

After much tugging, pushing, and moving of furniture, the rug was finally down. But our day of carnival had scarcely begun.

About four in the afternoon, two hours before the first guests were scheduled to arrive, David came in with the tables —all of which had to be assembled! Fortunately Neal and Ruth arrived shortly afterward, and Neal succeeded in setting them up in time for the evening. David brought in two of his lamps, and the room began to look more substantial.

The party was a most successful one, and everyone seemed to enjoy themselves. Enid and Kate and Ruth served as hostesses; Neal and Enid's husband, James, took care of the cocktails. Toward the end of the evening Mr. Salmon came over to me. "It was a wonderful party, Bob. Now that we're neighbors—I live in this section of Brooklyn, too—I hope you'll come and visit me sometime."

There is one problem that still remains unsolved for me, stemming from my deafness. It is impossible for me to hear my doorbell ring; consequently, I never know when a visitor arrives.

A friend, Harry Bell, has rigged a fan in such a way that, when a visitor presses a button at the door, the fan sets up a draft of air. But this system has definite limitations; I can only sense the draft from the fan if I am sitting beside the small table which holds it. If I am working in the kitchen or in another room, there is no way to reach me, no way of knowing that someone is calling.

Until now the only possible solution to this situation has

been to make special arrangements to leave my door un-locked when friends are coming. Or, if I expect them at a definite time, I seat myself near the table and wait for the fan to signal that they are at the door. Perhaps this is the most difficult problem for a deaf-blind person who lives alone; I still hope that some adequate solution will be found.

Initiating myself into the mysteries of the art of cooking has been one of my most pleasant—and sometimes unpleas-ant—chores. Good food, I soon learned, requires a good pilot to steer the ladle.

Breakfast is something of a bother, since it always comes at a time when I am in a hurry to shave and dress for the office. Keeping my beard out of my scrambled eggs is really a feat; holding a yolk in one hand and a razor in the other demands some degree of skill.

In my first attempts at cooking vegetables and meats I kept running back and forth to look into the pots, uncertain about the time required for cooking them. Once—and only once—I took a number of eggs from the fire, thinking that they were done, only to discover after breaking the shells that they were still raw.

Many recipes in my Braille cookbooks call for the white of egg or the yolk of egg. I solved this problem of the separation of parts by making a small aperture in the end of the shell; the whites run out into the bowl, and the yolks remain.

Cooking, I discovered, is like any other science; experi-mentation is the only road to success. Though my experi-ments have sometimes ended in utter cremations, these have not been as frequent as one would expect—much to my satisfaction. And cooking a dinner that friends enjoy is a most rewarding pastime.

In the beginning of my experiences as a cook, I purchased as much electrical equipment as I could find available—an electric frying pan, a pressure cooker, and an outsized mixer. Yet as my knowledge of preparing food grew, I seldom used these expensive items of kitchenware, preferring to use the ordinary gas range and assembly of pots and pans. These proved much easier to clean, as well as being less cumbersome and less demanding as far as space is concerned.

A friend suggested that I try cooking peas with a small amount of soda added to the cooking liquid. Perhaps I used too much; but before I knew it, I was picking peas from various nooks and crannies in my kitchen—under the stove, from the top of the kitchen counters, and everywhere.

Another friend suggested that I use an electric egg-cooker —the kind that uses a minimum of water and shuts itself off when all the water has boiled away. Already having decided that electrical things were more of a luxury and burden than a real boon to me, I never followed the advice. I discovered that cooking eggs to the right consistency is an art, however. I solved the problem by using the same pot with approximately the same amount of water every time; I turn the gas to just the right place on the dial, and time the cooking from the start. Of course, this required experimentation over a period of time—but it works!

That wonderful but somewhat unpredictable delicacy, the pancake, proved to be a genuine effort for me. Because the batter is so smooth, I found it difficult to judge the correct amount to use for each frying. Invariably I made the pancake too large, so that when I turned it, the large cartwheel broke and I was left with the problem of salvaging the pieces. And the first few times I made pancakes, I must admit they were of enormous size. I am not ashamed to admit, too, that my first one was hard enough to have been used for the flywheel of a machine.

My sense of proportion with regard to the amount of

food to prepare for a guest was acutely at fault from the very first day I felt courageous enough to invite a friend to dinner. Indiscriminately, I would heap the plates with food, hoping that I was not serving too small a portion. On one occasion when Harry Weitman came to dine he protested, "You know I eat very little—this is too much! Please—next time serve only half as much food."

I still remember the time I first made dumplings for a stew. Following the recipe, I inadvertently put too much soda in the mixture, and when I thought the stew was finished I dropped tablespoonfuls onto the simmering gravy. Ten minutes later I removed the cover from the pot. I sampled it. The dumplings had formed beautifully, but they had a strange acid taste that was definitely not agreeable. Furthermore, the misfortune had ruined the entire stew; it was my first really major fiasco in the kingdom of pots and pans.

One Saturday evening, after I had finally settled down to the art of housekeeping and felt comparatively self-assured, I invited several deaf friends to my apartment for a social visit. My old friends, Issy and Anna, were among them, and I was proud as I showed them through the rooms. Leaving my company in the living room, I busied myself in the kitchen, slicing meats, brewing coffee, and filling plates with olives and gherkins.

When we had begun to eat, Anna said "This coffee is delicious—really delicious!" My breast swelled with pride like that of a pouter pigeon: I felt so exhilarated by the compliment that I drank three cups of coffee myself. But as usual, I had overestimated the amount of food for the party; the dishes were still full of food after we had all gorged ourselves. I have always been mindful of that exacting proverb of the Puritans: "Unwarranted waste leads to woeful want"— but I have never been able to practice its moral.

Yes, when all is said and done, life has increased in charm and beauty with my appreciation of its richness, until even its less cheerful aspects have mellowed under my understanding. I have many interests which occupy my time. I have learned to be philosophical about my limitations, rather than selfish and bitter.

Loneliness was continually present in my life after I became deaf and blind. And even now, in adulthood, I find it with me despite all my adjustments to social living. Loneliness is a hunger for increasing human companionship, a need to be part of the activity that I know is constantly going on about me. And I feel that it is as necessary to human nature as sun and rain is to growing things. To share my moments of joy with someone else, to have others sympathize with my failures, appreciate my accomplishments, understand my moods and value my intelligence—these are the essential conditions that are needed for happiness. Praise alone does not fulfill this yearning for companionship; neither does sympathy. There must always be that bond of true personal interest which promotes an assurance that one is really wanted, not merely tolerated.

I believe that loneliness is not only a hunger for companionship; it is also a psychogenic need for other things that make life worth while—music, color, voices, faces and all the natural phenomena that are taken for granted by those who see and hear them constantly. I wish that I could hear the song of a bluebird as I watch it flitting through the fresh green life of spring; I wish that I could have the aesthetic pleasure of listening to Beethoven, Schubert, and the other great composers in their full, tonal glory; I wish that I could see the faces of the people with whom I speak and listen to their voices. I know that there is a glory of sound and beauty all around me, qualities of the senses of hearing and sight that my fingers cannot recognize or redeem through the sense of touch. To possess the world as it actually is in its fullness of measure, together with the solace of companionship, would be the highest zenith of joy. There would be no loneliness then; everything would have the completeness for which a human being has been made.

My need to voice these feelings has turned me increasingly to writing poetry. For poetry is the language which interprets the soul of living things. When the night wind carries the scent of flowers like a deep, soft breath, one knows that the darkness is living all about him and that the silence is filled with the potential music of the world. Out of this music grows a song for the years, a song strong in faith and happiness. I have written as I felt and thought—simply and sincerely and with great enjoyment, and quite without intent to offer my songs to others. I guard my memories. I keep them burnished bright that the faith of my heart, the work of my hands, and the laughter of my soul may continue to be fruitful of happiness. They have built for me courage into power and power into life.

And as I look ahead, I offer this prayer in the best way I know how to the Creator of hearing and of sight.

> Lord, give me courage and the grace to bear
> Life's tribulations with humility,
> That I may learn, through triumph and despair
> What happiness these simple things can be:
> To give without desiring to receive;
> To love without requiring to be loved;
> To revive faith in those who doubt or grieve;
> To move the heart that never has been moved.